Graphic Design Sources

**Dedicated to all the
students—not just those cited
in this book—who have
enriched my life,
the profession of graphic design,
and the lives of others**

Kenneth J. Hiebert

Graphic Design
sources

YALE UNIVERSITY PRESS
NEW HAVEN AND LONDON

Published with assistance from the Louis Stern
Memorial Fund.

This project was supported in part by a grant from
the National Endowment for the Arts, a federal
agency.

Library of Congress
Cataloging-in-Publication Data

Hiebert, Kenneth J.
Graphic design sources / Kenneth J. Hiebert.
     p.   cm.
Includes bibliographical references.
ISBN 0–300–07461–1 (cloth:alk. paper)
1. Graphic arts—Technique. 2. Computer-aided
design. 3. Computer graphics—Technique.
4. Graphic design (Typography)
I. Title.
NC1000.H55 1998
741.6—dc21

                        97–34826
                           CIP

A catalogue record for this book is available from
the British Library.

The paper in this book meets the guidelines for
permanence and durability of the Committee
on Production Guidelines for Book Longevity of
the Council on Library Resources.

10 9 8 7 6 5 4 3 2 1

Contents

Drawing from . . .

For me, venturing into other domains has always been intriguing. Interpretive information design always involves crossing boundaries, drawing from other sources.

A major additional stimulus to do a sequel to *Graphic Design Processes . . . universal to Unique,* with similar grounding in the universal, has come from the media deluge that makes it nearly impossible to make something new. It is now, more than ever, much easier to parody than to create a new form. Media saturation gives us consciousness before experience. Today, what you see is already old by the time you see it. The challenge for educators is to be "with it"—Zeitgeist-oriented in some fundamental sense— without being merely trendy. Emerson's notion that "perpetual modernness is the measure of merit in every work of art," implying that something both durable and new can always be found, is harder and harder to realize.

So I was very pleased to have the National Endowment for the Arts identify this ongoing concern—to dig beyond the stylistic to more essential qualities—as a subject worthy of funding. I wish hereby to gratefully acknowledge the support of peers in the NEA review process.

This book is the composite of the work of many students in addition to my own investigations. I regret only that not more could be shown of the beautiful, inventive, and dynamic work of my students, by now a huge treasure store. Those whose work has been used are listed in the Credits at the back of the book.

Armin Hofmann, to whom I am most indebted for his paradigmatic instruction and example during and since my time at the Basel School of Design, has kindly added his words in a Foreword.

Christine Hiebert has been terrifically helpful in sorting out chapters 1 and 7. These two, for me both more difficult and exhilarating chapters than the others, draw from the natural and frame the rest of the subjects which draw from the human-created.

My wife, Eleanor, has added chapter manuscripts of this book to her already heavy bag of music scores on her commute by bus and subway to bring her own demand for simple clarity to bear on the text. I cannot thank her enough for both this tangible support and the less tangible and ubiquitous one on a spiritual level.

I am indebted to the University of the Arts and the Graphic Design Department for the environment of faculty and students within which I have been able to freely pursue my teaching activity. Inge Druckrey, William Longhauser, and Richard Felton all gave valuable comments on the Introduction.

Finally—and certainly not least—I am indebted to Judy Metro of Yale University Press for her persistent enthusiasm in supporting the publication of *Graphic Design Sources.* The staff's efforts in assuring the quality of the enterprise, especially that of Laura Jones Dooley, the manuscript editor for this volume, and Mary Mayer, who has overseen the production, added much to its final quality.

In *Graphic Design Sources* Ken Hiebert delves deeply into those complex questions that absorb us more and more in the arena of visual communication. Techniques springing from electronic media combined with new thought processes permit a much freer handling of visually perceived elements than heretofore. The emergence of new, multifaceted word and picture forms opens the way to a fundamental change from the ones to which we have become accustomed.

Even though the underlying factors and theories of the new languages of form are a subject of widespread intellectual investigation, the translation of more theoretical research into tangibly useful terms is not only lacking but inadequate in and of itself to penetrate the new communication phenomena. Teaching structures that more effectively link research with concrete, formative processes are needed in schools of communication design. The professional education of graphic designers has frequently been jeopardized by an unnecessary schism between more intellectual and more intuitive and perceptual educational approaches. Today, in the circumstances precipitated by the functioning of mass media in society, this separation is both educationally and socially-politically precarious.

These considerations have undoubtedly led Ken Hiebert to develop teaching and learning structures in which this problem is addressed—in which research and expression can be accomplished as a whole. In seven chapters, significant themes in contemporary graphic design are thoroughly treated. Almost filmlike in the sequencing, the network of factors woven into design processes is made visible and clarified. Especially interesting are probes in the lifting of the typographic into the visual realm. The way conventional boundaries between and among pictures, signs, words, numbers, and color values can be altered and expanded to achieve shifts in meaning is impressively documented.

Semiotics—the language of signs—is a main underlying, if not stated, theme of the book.

Not least, Hiebert also points to drawing as being of continuing central importance in education. Although he constantly acknowledges the influence and significance of new technologies in today's education, the question of the essential sources for creative, formative work is posed over and over again. The observation of nature, attention to natural formal development, interest in the exposition of our visually perceptible environment—these are self-evident conditions and anchor points for the development of a graphic designer. The pencil retains its perennial importance at the beginning of the path. This can be deduced as clearly from the book as can its unreserved commitment to the renewal of visual means of expression.

Armin Hofmann

*"Study is a searching in everything,
in the smallest, in the most hidden, in good and bad.
Then somehow a light ignites, and a single right way is pursued."*

—Paul Klee

The Reality of Graphic Design

Graphic Design Is Interface Design

In the largest sense, all graphic design serves as an interface. It is the filter that facilitates communication between users and products, places, processes, information, and services. This interface may have the purpose of description or persuasion. It may be in a process of one-way presentation or two-way discourse (interactive). It has a functional rather than a decorative purpose.

In current usage, interface design most often refers to the screen image of a computer through which layers of information are made accessible. This should be considered a specific type of interface.

Graphic design is thus ubiquitous because every product or communication that is exchanged requires an interface. If you don't like a design, you basically don't like the interface between you and the content.

Graphic Design Is Interdisciplinary

Graphic design provides access to information of any kind.

Perhaps it is the interdisciplinary quality of graphic design that makes it so difficult to explain. On one hand, we manage a variety of images—typography, maps and charts, photographs, illustrations—each with its own complex histories, technologies, and cultures. We deal with color, texture, sound, and motion. We manage a wide range of applications and formats, each with its own histories, technologies, and cultures: stationery and forms, books, posters, catalogs, product information, banners, identity programs, environmental graphics, and time-based multimedia. With each project we function in a cultural context with economic constraints and economic goals. Our projects are the result of extensive planning. They involve complex questions of production, of translation of idea and form into reproducible form. Not least, we confront in each project different content and purpose. Because graphic interpretation is so complex, it is little

wonder that clients look for track records (styles!) and specialization to assure results and allay the nervousness inherent in making huge investments.

Because, in the words of Jeanne Bamberger, "we can only know what we have bounded" (see chapter 4, Personal Experience Mapping), we all easily resort to the way we have bounded things in the past. This brings us to

the styles dilemma:
Pro . . .

Style when defined as the élan, the spirit with which something is said, done, expressed, or performed, is certainly a desirable goal. Style when defined as the distinctive features of visual expression is something that our work should yield. Style as a measure of consistency in usage—spelling, grammar (whether verbal or visual) —is indispensable to a social existence.

. . . and con

Style as either the fashion of the moment—the chic, the craze, the rage—or the worn conventions and traditions that result from habitual usage, carries dangers for the creative person or team because in each case it is the finished style that lures. This lure can subvert the authentic search that originates in process and counters the preconceived result. It is easier to parody than to "birth" a new form.

Each new problem and its interdisciplinary framework has inherent potential for unique form and content; each problem has its own dynamic from which we can draw.

Interdisciplinary implies discipline

Work that crosses disciplines without training in at least one specific discipline can easily yield the effect of complexity at the expense of the requisite depth, cogency, and meaning.

Conversely, an attachment to the tradition of a discipline can have an atrophying effect. The challenge is to develop discipline but stay alive

"Judging this show left me with a rule of thumb about design: a great designer is one who gets his or her inspiration from anything other than the work of his or her contemporaries and rivals and furthermore, is skillful enough to use inspiration in a way that isn't derivative. Period."
—Karrie Jacobs

to the new and evolving.

Establishing a deeply rooted discipline has to do with having time to contemplate things until they reveal their mystery and presence, being able to build from scratch without relying on stylistic patinas, trusting a process, melding craft and concept, not seeing from one side only, and learning to be honest in work and social relationships.

Contrast this with a "fun thing" as defined by a neighbor after his wife complimented him on how great his temporary sod looked. He replied, "It's just an idea—it won't work. It's just a fun thing. It'll look good for a while, but it's full of weeds . . . . But it's better than mud."

Full of weeds. It won't last.

Graphic Design Crosses Boundaries

Although several functions of image production in graphic design are now merged in a single tool, the computer—giving the designer greater power, freedom, and responsibility—the design of most projects are collaborations among other designers, writers, editors, photographers, illustrators, clients, account executives, producers, software designers, printers, and others. In this multidisciplinary milieu, it is possible to function well as a specialist with a limited contribution to the conceptual work of a project. Although such graphic technicians are needed, the designer is one who can cross boundaries, whose sense of the whole and contribution toward it is fundamental to achieving graphic clarity.

Boundary crossing is essential . . . and healthy

Crossing boundaries—discovering the application of one experience of life to another—is the basis for many of the greatest discoveries. It is the basis for a satisfying and exhilarating life, the mark of a healthy human existence. It is the basis for understanding ecology, without which we cannot survive the exploitation of overspecialization.

Think of the impact of outsiders: Jane

Jacobson on city planning, Marshall McLuhan on media understanding, Luis Barragan on architecture, Rachel Carson on science, the artist in India who turned from making votive objects for Hindu temples to making sensationally effective, inexpensive, and fast-to-fit artificial legs and said he is happier being a social worker than an entertainer.

Specialization, by contrast, contributes to that immaturity that makes us part of an arrogant, myopic, and excessively bounded clique that thinks it is complete, that leads to a kind of narcissism in which you worship yourself in a group. Encounters across boundaries mean taking risks and drawing from new associations. Coming out of our parochial existence is the way to insight and generosity, to comparisons that put experience in perspective.

Our delight and purpose as form-givers is to expect and embrace the unexpected, to give us the versatility to enter new situations, to make discoveries. To achieve surprise, the temptation—indeed, the need—to mix forms unexpectedly is always there. Mixing means crossing boundaries: from one medium to another, from one domain of knowledge to another, from one mode of expression to another, from one mood to another, from one time period to another, from one color palette to another, and so on.

In crossing boundaries we are in effect layering experience. For a layering experience to be illuminating, each plane needs clarity and form; otherwise the tendency will be toward occlusion rather than opening, toward density rather than vitality.

For each layer to have a mature form means that it is the product of history, experience, and insight. When we look across boundaries to another domain we are tempted to think that we could do that activity, too. From the perspective of graphic design, it might look as though we could jump into fabric design or ceramics or whatever else with little difficulty. Yet when we try it we realize that there is a special discipline, a special history, a special world that we can't

enter quite as easily as we thought. Being grounded in a discipline, though, lets us comprehend the special domain of another and prepares us, if not to fuse it, then to be its interpreter, its interface.

Education as a Strategy of Preparation for Professional Practice

School can be a very real world—potentially more deeply real than much of the so-called real world. If school is not that, it is missing its calling as a special place where very important and *ultimately practical experiences* are gained—experiences that can't be had on the job. At their best, these experiences are equipment for life.

What could be more real than this?

A good and vital education promotes durable values, including these:

1. Understanding versus deception

"In an ideal speech act," Jim Thomas tells us, *"understanding is based on several cultural assumptions. Among the most important are the presumptions that the speaker and audience possess mutual competency (there are no private languages) and there is no intent to deceive. However, in the real world, especially one in which deceptive manipulation of symbols offers a useful resource, these assumptions break down. In everyday life, deceit, private languages, veiled meanings, communicative incompetence, differing interpretive abilities and other factors mediate how identity is formulated, culture is understood, and behavioral responses are chosen and implemented. . . .*

"[Manipulating] symbols to one's own advantage subverts 'authentic communication' by requiring some successful messages to depend on equally successful deception or concealment of other agendas that inhibit understanding.

"The goal of communication is coming to a mutually reciprocal understanding through the meaningful exchange of symbols. Repressive communication refers to obstructions either in symbol creation or exchange."

The milieu for social application of design, like the electoral process, is frustrating because of insensitivity, ignorance, noninvolvement, and cynicism about the believability of it all.

In the conflict between intrinsic value and manipulated value, the first concern in education is understanding the intrinsic. A genuine encounter with the substance of a thing or idea of worth and the pursuit of understanding over deception is the best antidote to cynicism. Authenticity and honesty are high goals with lasting outcomes.

2. Root concepts and structure

Concepts are tools for defining relationships. At root level, relationships can be represented in the most primary visual terms. For graphic design these include the vocabulary of visual language: point, line, and plane; modules, sets, and rhythm; scale, dimensionality, and proportion; texture, pattern, and color; symbol and metaphor.

Professions go to "root particles" in research. Often in schools—and out of schools—come new discoveries and advances. This is true for medicine, physics, engineering, economics, and music. It should be true for design. Paradoxically, the renewal of a profession often comes from a return to basics. . . .

"To learn structure is to learn how things are related. The teaching and learning of structure, rather than simply the mastery of facts and technique, is at the center of the classic problem of transfer. . . . Perhaps the most basic thing that can be said about human memory . . . is that unless detail is placed into a structured pattern, it is rapidly forgotten."—Jerome Bruner

To be able to push a formal idea back to the point at which it can be identified as a rule with transformational power is an accomplishment of the utmost importance, for once so equipped a student is able to revert to the simplest of ideas and generate new aspects of it for new purposes. Without transfer, education is a waste.

"People are beginning to understand that the wave of decorative uselessness that dominated the eighties was a 'closed' style that led nowhere. . . . If a design's end result isn't useful, then you have to call its whole nature into question. . . . So it's back to basics. Reduced and uncomplicated is suddenly refreshing, even liberating."
—Jasper Morrison

3. Universals link

The more universal and essential, the more susceptible forms are to usefulness

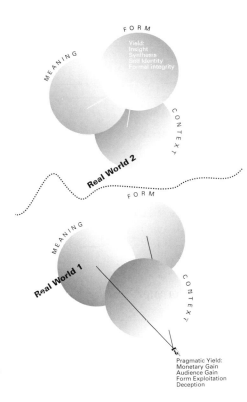

The diagram shows the relation of Real World 1, with its emphasis on context— often at the expense of form—to Real World 2, where the elements of form and meaning are preeminent. Form gives graphic design its buoyancy; context brings it down to earth. Reconciling the two domains is real world work.

beyond boundaries. The complaint that universals alienate or that distillation to essentials robs a form of contextual relevance is valid only when the grounding in universals is not coupled with the unique aspects of a site (architecture) or message (graphic design).

An architectural entrance thought of as an aperture or gateway (universal, inclusive) rather than as an architectural style (specific, exclusionary) will connect conceptually to other openings, such as how a graphic communication is "entered."

The eminent designer and educator Armin Hofmann has the vision for the potential of the basic and universal elements of communication, but also the feeling and stamina to imbue pristine elements with new qualities stemming uniquely from content and sites. He achieves a synthesis of both archaic-primal and eminently modern qualities in the sense that, as Ralph Waldo Emerson stated, "Perpetual modernness is the measure of merit in every work of art."

4. Connection to ourselves

"Our senses find slick products to be disconnected from the invisible inner life. There is no palpable comprehension of the meaning of these things. This loss of reality in things touches the central nerve of connectedness, which till now has been the essence of design."

This statement implies that many slick, supposedly "real" mass-produced products actually alienate, are disconnected from our inner selves and senses, and therefore lack *fundamental* reality. Yet they are the product of so-called real-world processes, including marketing! The "real world" is not such a good training ground after all.

Graphic design at its best avoids being merely a functionary in the creation of apparently diverse but actually redundant images or products. Instead it reveals authentically sensed diversity. If we connect to form and content, giving meaning through tangibly based perception, feeling, and making —our own passionate connection—

we have a chance to make things of value.

5. Holistic seeing

There is a way of looking at anything to see it both as a whole and in its detail.

Two aspects that contribute to holistic seeing, which the real world neglects and good education supplies, are:
1. Seeing things simultaneously as abstract form *and* as content. This increases exponentially our ability to create relationships—the essence of design.
2. Using and understanding *space as counterform* instead of as a background or stylistic device.

The time required to learn and comprehend these broader dimensions of form are usually not available in pragmatic situations. Yet they are key factors that distinguish aesthetically strong and timeless imagery.

6. Expression versus effect

Expression is the goal of communication. It should not be confused with mere effect. If dominant, an effect may have an entertainment value that will distract from the expression.

With Louis Kahn, I am a modernist, in the sense that our creations are shrines for ideas, acts, feelings, and perceptions.

"For Kahn, a library was not a place for storage and circulation, nor the occasion for a flamboyant formal gesture. It was a shrine to the human act of learning, a shrine . . . imbued with silence and light. His architecture, like Corbusier's, did not need to rely on classical models."

Kahn was not afraid to assert the mystical qualities of materials, to go beyond material to the naming of qualities hidden in it. Modernists had to reinvent the spiritual because the notion of the Supreme had been trivialized. Modernism, when perceived this way, is neither sterile nor outmoded. And postmodernism, by claiming a connection to classical tradition, easily slips into the fallacy of quotation substituting for actual experience.

Real-world experiences often rob us of a complete experience. Often we are doing only pieces of pieces. A satisfy-

"Memory has no taste for noise; it needs a message."
—Jeremy Campbell

ing extent of realization is a rarity, not only for most designers but for most people. The division of labor in design often results in the application of effects by someone other than the originator. Performance is separated from its origins.

"Performing is not creative . . . . Performers are like talking dogs. Some of them are very intelligent, but you'd be amazed at how uninformed some of our greatest performers can be about music, not to mention the other arts."—Ned Rorem

What about design?

7. Developing dynamic duality

Form is not a dogma; it can spring freely from content or from working, from being alive. But aliveness alone as construed in the postmodern "New Academy"—as open-ended, free associative layering—without potent duality, misses. Duality is the essential, dynamic contrast that creates the reliable, fresh context for meaning. It lies at the heart of the examples in this book.

In the world of images and ideas the constraints on hybridization that exist for animal or plant species don't exist. As Stefan Wolpe eloquently stated in his homage to Dada, "All things are in the reach of the human mind and . . . to connect is a mental act." But the permission to connect is tempered by the basis for perceiving connection—namely, adjacency and contrast. The definition of opposites provides a vital context and control for conveying meaning. Contrast allows for a connection that isn't arbitrary. Though I might connect anything internally, only if this connection is perceived as such is it useful for communication.

8. Transparency

In Italo Calvino's *Six Memos for the Next Millennium,* Lightness, Quickness, Exactitude, Visibility, Multiplicity, and Consistency are prized as supreme values. It is not enough merely to list them; each is interpreted relative to the range created by its opposite, and Calvino's elucidation of these values is worth reading.

To these I would add *transparency.* In listening to a musical work, especially one involving multiple instruments, it is a sign, at least for me, of an engaging performance to hear both the overall line of the music and the voices that comprise it. That is, there is layering, but not covering. Transparency, not opacity. The denser the music, the more the danger of a thick, muddied execution. In the classic dynamic contrast of concealing and revealing—though the two are mutually dependent—revealing is nevertheless the more valued. We are allowed to look into rather than at. In transparency we are searching and assembling from the layers. Our acuity is greater and with it our interest and involvement.

9. Inward/outward—micro/macro/micro

A rhythm of turning inward to a micro world in which we are in control but where we seek new form and new life across old boundaries and turning outward to bring our experience to social relevance—this is for me an ideal.

All our activity is a flux between these poles, the poles of looking inward and looking outward, of crossing these boundaries.

Rightness of design is not an absolute. The condition of dynamic tension between literalness and abstraction, between individual and society, between quality and pragmatic compromise, is one of "hovering rightness"—not a fixed point but a state of flux within a progressively more focused zone.

10. Building practical idealism and flexibility with play

Besides a grounding in some primary discipline, crossovers require flexibility and delight in discovery of connections.

"The secret of flexible behavior is to have interesting experiences in stable conditions as free as possible from serious danger. One of the most important of these is play. Play, which is the normal activity of children who feel secure, is a symptom of versatility that tends to lead to more versatility. Play is a symbolic activity. . . . its

"Our great mistake is to exact from each person virtues which he does not possess, and to neglect the cultivation of those which he has."
—Hadrian

rules may be broken, or new rules invented,
without leading to serious consequences. . . .
In play it is possible to go to extremes,
to be daring, to experiment, so that the
practical can be tested to the full."
—Jeremy Campbell

10. Perfectionism and failure

Failure is a way to overcome fear. Climbing among rocks you may feel afraid and stressfully cautious. You slip and recover and are reassured by the accident because you know more about the terrain and how it behaves. Rightly conceived, education allows for risk and failure as essential steps toward greater perfection.

Crossing boundaries means to become disoriented, even lost, but only until a new and greater synthesis is found.

11. Poetry

What I mean by a poetic aesthetic, an aesthetic of rhythmic crossover, is, I hope, substantiated in this book of demonstrations. Poetry should not be confused with sentimentality or sweetness. Rather it is a cutting through that reveals essences.

The Changing Environment

Creating kinesis in space has been the modernist goal; the new realities that graphic designers face are those of converting space to time, combining images, text, and sound in a time-based medium.

The digital image platform and multimedia enable the convergence of disciplines in startling new ways, yielding a rich complexity of interaction. It requires also the realization that, as Jeremy Campbell so aptly states, *"Complexity is not just a matter of a system having a lot of parts which are related to one another in nonsimple ways. Instead it turns out to be a special property in its own right, and it makes complex systems different in kind from simple ones, enabling them to do things and be things we might not have expected."*

Preparation for cross-media work is the seeing of relations in a matrixlike configuration rather than as a linear sequence, whether these are presented as a two-dimensional printed piece, a three-dimensional construction, or a multimedia screen image.

Life Is a Matrix

Matrix:
    source, womb
    place of nurture
    web, network

As a womb, a matrix can be thought of as a situation or surrounding substance within which something else originates, develops, or is contained. As a web or network, in the sense used here, a matrix is the constantly enlarging fabric of experience in which things intersect to create new combinations. A matrix can be thought of as a meeting place for all kinds of diversity. Invention can be seen as the particular and unique combination of things nurtured within the matrix, crossing boundaries to form a new combination.

Life is a matrix. It takes time to build the network of experiences that provide the basis for crossover. We must always be reaching across boundaries crossed in ourselves. Then we can better find and understand the dynamic contrasts in any situation and build effective, involving communication. Building a matrix requires trust in the accretions of time and a commitment to lifelong curiosity and education.

In this book, graphic form-giving is sought by looking across boundaries into other domains. This is more than looking for inspiration. It is opening ourselves to a larger world and a larger vision.

It is not a how-to-do book, a formula for doing things.

It's about how to think about the process of doing. You will have your own explorations and discoveries.

Drawing from . . .

Nature

Nature as a source, symbolized most by the earth and our solar system—its structure and composition, its genesis, its organisms, its processes and dynamism, its cyclical energy, its diversity, complexity, and interconnectedness, its nourishment for life, its wonders and terror, its surprises amid its rhythmic periodicity, its vastness, its invisible forces—is inexhaustible. Nature gives us our bearings, our reference points, our sensory apparatus to apprehend its phenomena, and the intelligence to respond to it and to use it.

This chapter introduces key ways in which nature serves as source and stimulus. A structure for understanding the continuum of created form from literal to abstract is presented and an image exploration using this information is developed.

> *"A little closer to the heart of creation than usual, yet not nearly close enough."*
>
> —*Paul Klee*

Nature as Source and Reference

There is for me nothing more rejuvenating and restorative than a walk through woods or along the seashore. Yet I do not think of nature as only the idyllic natural, though it includes this. Nature is the ongoing process of evolution and creation, the confluence of myriad forces in constant dynamic interplay. Our views of nature are typically static slices from what is alternately terrifying and serene, ominous and benign, infinity and finitude, life and death. Using nature as a model means recognizing forces at work. By drawing from nature, we are not going to a static or wholly predictable source. Extracting beautiful form from nature—unless the definition of beautiful includes the terrifying and the unknown—is a limited view. Our problem is in seeing nature and knowing our place in it and our relation to it.

Elements or aspects of the natural world visible to the naked eye seem eminently useful for communication. History or specialized knowledge is not required. A general, shared, overwhelming sense of the natural, of the earth and our belonging to it, makes nature an ideal basis for common understanding.

But is literal representation of nature a good vehicle to communicate meaning? The painter Paul Klee's yearning to know nature more deeply has to be seen in the light of his knowing that it is part of the human experience to look for meaning beneath the surface (see also the quotation on page 32).

We find meaning in natural processes, but paradoxically, focusing a meaning requires getting away from a literal representation. At the mythological extreme, societies most closely connected to nature represent their belief systems in nonliteral, nonnaturalistic terms. Although artifacts of symbolic expression may be "organic" in the sense of being carved from and respecting wood as a source, for example, the forms are typically a reproportioning unique to the abstracting ability of the maker or the maker's society. But at the other extreme, the scientific one, the depiction of natural structures and processes often requires enhancement to achieve clarity, whether in the assigning of color or form, the choice of viewpoint, or other means to dramatize.

John Dewey's description of the evolution of meaning, the miracle of communication, and the ultimate contrast between events in nature and their representation in the mind once they are named is a cogent description of this process. He explains that when things or events take on meaning, they acquire signs and surrogates that are easier to manage, more flexible and more permanent at the same time, than in their original state. We cannot duplicate nature, but we can bring nature to a state of symbolic power that is a purely human accomplishment.

"Of all affairs, communication is the most wonderful. That things should be able to pass from the plane of external pushing and pulling to that of revealing themselves to man, and thereby to themselves; and that the fruit of communication should be participation, sharing; is a wonder by the side of which transubstantiation pales."

Communication is an artificial world. As the extent of the artificial world increases, we look for ways to bring the artifacts we create into a harmonic relationship akin to nature. Yet the further we go toward imitating nature, the further we go toward a futile goal. Even the literal registering of nature using photography is finally elusive. Lens, light, film, viewpoint, scale, finished surface—all comport to create a momentary, and thus already an inherently unique and specific, departure from nature.

Nature combines more factors than we can ever dream of synthesizing. Duplicating nature in the forms we use for communication is neither possible nor desirable. More

---

Observations while pruning raspberries:

There are two kinds of canes: spent canes and one-year canes. At a glance, the whole patch looks the same. How will the canes be sorted? Besides being relatively brittle and dead, the spent canes give another clue: they have branched. The new canes have usually not branched but have sent all their energy into one stem. I think of spent ideas, of things that are exhausted, where the branching has reached a limit. I think of the "unbreakable cup" series in my book "Graphic Design Processes." It branches to a point of dissipation that is reached just after the most profuse fruition.

I have called this "going to seed"—worth nothing more in its current life. The new cane doesn't branch until it has built up energy and strength. Viewpoints are like that; work in which we are fully invested is like that. It takes time to gather and concentrate our forces. Then I see that I am walking through clumps of rabbit dung. The raspberries are being fertilized without my effort. The heavier cover of the raspberry patch has drawn the animals. Scattered around, I now notice, are blue jay feathers—one of the neighborhood cats has probably brought about the bird's demise. All these are signs of the cyclical in nature, and to imagine that this dead-looking patch of sticks is going to supply scrumptious weekend brunches for another year is beyond the wildest human imagination.

Dormancy is essential to the process.

16

honest and authentic is a reaction to nature from an individual human perspective, a specific translation of the experience of nature.

Drawing from nature is a process of extraction—isolating something, bounding it, taming it; of realizing its wild origins while finding a way to interpret it.

The extraction process is contextual, but just behind our formal inquiry lies the ideal of nature. We can think of nature as having qualities that give criteria for our work as form-givers to artifacts of culture. A catalog of these qualities and their importance as sources begins on page 18. This in itself is a process of abstraction. The examples then show a further step of abstraction, "drawing from."

A cognitive map of the cosmos by the Siberian Chuckchi society. The form is related to natural forms with a nexus, such as flowers or webs, and the subject is human relation to the rest of nature, but the particular arrangement is interpretive out of intuition— an abstraction functioning symbolically.

A garden of objects

Today we live in a world of objects designed for rapid consumption, objects requiring a minimum of effort and attention to use them, but also objects that leave no lasting impression on our memories— a throw-away world that requires no effort but, at the same time, produces no real quality.
Now imagine a garden with flowers and fruit trees. Think of the attention, time, and energy required and think of the results: flowers and fruit. For those who have grown them, value cannot be measured in banally economic terms. Of course, a garden should produce flowers and fruit, but the person tending it does so for a more general reason— love of the plants. Now try to imagine an analogous relationship between objects. Think of objects that are beautiful and useful as trees in your own garden, objects that endure and have lives of their own—objects that perform services and require care.
If the more general role of design is to produce images of an inhabitable world, one way is to propose criteria of quality that have as reference points the garden and the care that it requires. I am thinking of criteria for quality that lead to a system of objects that have the variety, complexity, life, and blend of beauty and utility of a garden but, at the same time, are a product of the real world, a world extensively and intensively artificial.
It isn't simple; following this indication implies overturning the way design traditionally is more highly regarded than production. It implies an inversion of the relationship between subjects and objects. It implies a purposive consciousness that profoundly redefines the sense of its goals. It implies a new ecological sensibility—caring for objects can be a way of caring for that larger object that is our planet.
—Ezio Manzini

Nature is:
structural, expressed in increments and systems

Natural forms are composed of incremental systems of units, growing in successive steps.

The logarithms of shell growth are the basis for proportional systems in architecture and typography.
The ratios stemming from these growth patterns, such as the golden section or the Fibonaccian series (1, 1, 2, 3, 5, 8, 13, 21, . . . in which each number is the sum of the previous two and the growing surface or volume thus remains in each incremental step related to the previous one) are considered "ideal" because of their internal unity.

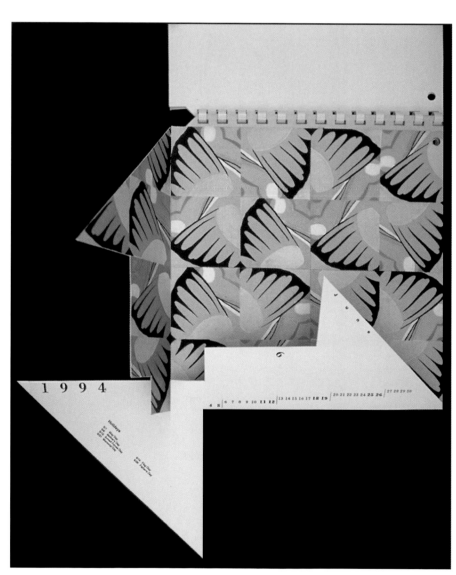

1 9 9 4

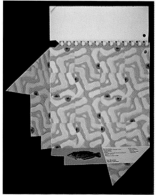

Patterns derived from tropical fish for a calendar.

Nature is:
diverse, expressed in variation within species

No two snowflakes, no fingerprints, no feathers are the same.

Differentiation in nature is a source of endless fascination. The variety in unity found in nature keeps our sensory organs alert and moving, scanning.

This "library of letter forms" for a building sign calls special attention to the letter form most related to the word *book* and varies the form of the letter according to its rhythmic occurrence in the word structure.

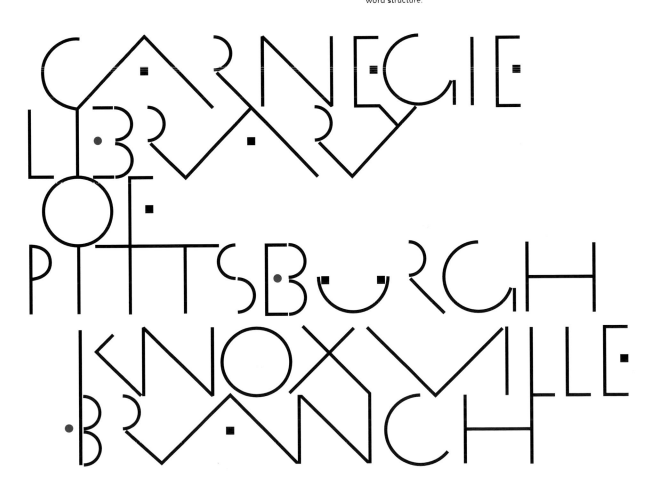

CARNEGIE LIBRARY OF PITTSBURGH KNOXVILLE BRANCH

Nature is:
vast, expressed in sheer expanse and depth

Whether looking inward to the world of underlying particles,
toward the larger landscape, or outward to the universe,
spatial depth is created endlessly.

Any vista that shows
us the near and the
distant reminds us of the
depth of the evolved
world.

The crossing of mes-
sages in space is a
human ideal that strives
to match our sense of
interlinked entities in the
natural world.

Nature is:
mysterious, expressed by invisible forces and interconnections

Forces beyond either our reach or grasp make us concede that much of nature is unknown or inexplicable.

The confluence of natural forces yields mysteries that intrigue and elude us.

Chance operations in image production, such as this interpretation of the Cowardly Lion from the *Wizard of Oz* (inside he's all mushy) relinquish partial control to the way things happen naturally.

I'm really just a coward

Nature is:
evolutionary, expressed in adaptivity

Nature is inventive, yielding species proliferation and mutation.

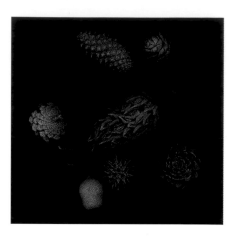

This array of pine cone variations only touches the surface in showing the actual range of form, each being a condition of adaptation to climate, terrain, and competition.

Type forms available in profusion as fonts, while exciting in their variety, are worthless unless the adaptation of any given form to its purpose makes it viable.
In this logotype for an association of mutual aid societies, choices are made in terms of strength, motion, historicity, and community to give the mélange of form a natural fitting together.

Nature is:
organic, expressed in eco-logic

Within organisms, the connectedness of parts in vital and essential relationship is awesomely demonstrated; among organisms and forces, ecological balancing of forces creating an organic wholeness is evident.

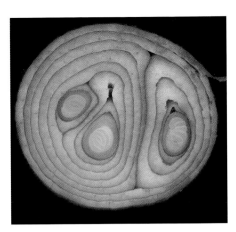

"Constituting an integral part of a whole; funda-mental" is one definition of the word *organic*. We see it dramatically in the successive rings of growth in a slice of onion, and within the rings, the precursors of the sprouting phase.

Organic form is the stimulus and the expression in this lithograph by Hans Arp. By isolating this quality from all the other levels of complexity, Arp reveals the form as truly human-made, yet with an authentic connection to nature.

Does *organic* mean *curved?* This is a common conception. The fluidity of the curvilinear form makes an obvious connection to natural forms. The Ornamine logo uses a contrast between curvi-linear and straight forms to create an "organic" transition from clogged to open and dry. This drug is an antihistamine to combat congestion. It is specifically a four-season drug, so the four-part rhythms are "organically" —in the larger sense of connoting wholeness— connected to the product's purpose.

Nature is:
dynamic, expressed in movement

Nature is in action; action is a sign of vitality. The velocity
  changes, but the fact of motion is pervasive.

Layers of clouds reveal
variations in wind velocity.

Music exists only in the
moment, giving way to
successive change. This
visual interpretation of
music in two-dimensional
space, a work by Gustav
Mahler, is an attempt to
create a visual equivalent
constantly in flux, like
nature.

Nature is:
culminating, expressed in climactic fruition

Natural processes are often consummated in a process
with peaks of maturation and perfection accompanied by
dramatic display of form and color.

The lore of nature is
replete with examples of
slow maturation or
gestation and magnificent,
climactic, short-lived,
ecstatic display, usually
coupled with the function
of attracting whatever
is required for the species'
continued existence.
We see it all the time in
flowers, but taken for
granted in the florist's
stunning arrangement is
the long preceding
period of development.

Ecstasy is a word reserved
in our culture for the
lurid, for bars and lounges
that may be the opposite!
But the ecstatic is a
natural human emotion
without which life is
incomplete. The emotional
high may be a rare
experience as it is in the
life of natural organisms,
but it is precisely this
rarity that gives ecstasy its
glow.

Nature is:
complex, expressed in strata of form

Each layer of natural reality is superimposed on another
to extremes of which it is humanly difficult to conceive.
Even at the surface level, natural forms mix into
a confounding complexity of texture and pattern.

While each leaf or other
piece of natural "debris"
in this picture is in itself
highly complex, the
extravagance of more or
less chaotic mixing is
typical of what we often
see in nature's wildness.
A coherency can also
be seen to transcend the
apparent chaos.

The dazzling complexity of
nature invites us to try
to use it when appropriate
to make a point in com-
munication. The erratic
rising of some letter forms
out of a mass gives a
clamoring character to the
word *dialogue* in a context
of discourse.

Nature is:
metamorphic, expressed in dramatic change

It transforms matter from one state to another unrecognizable
  one, from seed to plant, from caterpillar to butterfly,
  from egg to chicken, from embryo to human.

The potency of microscopic cell material to carry DNA is impressively displayed in the process of species reproduction where the information that determines the form is carried in ways unique to the species' environment, such as these twirling, winged maple seeds.

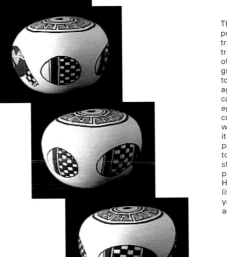

The Native American seed pot out of the Acoma tradition is a magnificent translation of the miracle of transformational growth from seed (egg) to growth. Though the age-old question of which came first, chicken or egg, pervades pragmatic culture, the more in-tune-with-earth view accepts it as an endless natural process and is able to communicate it with stunning clarity while preserving its mystery. Having turned this little seed pot around, one yearns to see it again, and again.

 27

Nature is:
cyclical, expressed in rhythmic periodicity
This is the predictable, sustaining aspect upon which we
depend. It is the systematic background of occurrences that
in human terms is desirable and fragile.

The holy sages of ancient China surveyed all the puzzling diversities under heaven. They observed forms and phenomena and made collections of linear signs to be used as oracles to represent those phenomena and their attributes. Through observations and discussion they perfected the changes and transformations of the things in the world of phenomena.

First there was the Great Primal Beginning. This generated the two primary forms: a continuous line called *yang*, symbol of the male, or positive, principle, and a divided line called *yin*, symbol of the female, or negative, principle. These are the basic symbols used in *The Book of Changes*. Combining yang and yin in various ways, they generated the four images:

old or great yang

young or little yang

old or great yin

young or little yin

Another line was then added to form eight trigrams.

These eight trigrams were held to represent all that happens in heaven and on earth. They were also held to be in a state of continual transition, one changing into another, just as the transition from one phenomenon to another is constant in the physical world. The eight trigrams are the fundamental unit of *The Book of Changes*.

The Book of Changes furthers the intuitive understanding of conditions in the world, penetrating to the utmost depths of nature and spirit. The eight trigrams create complete images of conditions and relations in the world. They intermingle in the unseen world, and their movements create an image that shows every event in the visible world.

The first trigram consists of three unbroken lines that symbolize creative primal power, which is light-giving, active, strong, and of the spirit. Because it is without weakness, its essence is power or energy. Its image is Heaven, and it represents the father in the family structure. Its energy is represented as unrestricted and is conceived of as motion. Because time is regarded as the basis of this motion, it also includes the power of time and the power of persisting in time—that is, duration.

The second trigram consists of three broken lines that represent the dark, yielding, receptive primal power of earth. The attribute of the trigram is devotion; its image is Earth, and it represents mother. Earth is the perfect complement of the Creative. Heaven— the complement, not the opposite—for the Receptive does not combat the Creative but completes it. Earth represents nature in contrast to spirit, Earth in contrast to heaven, space as against time, the female-maternal as against the male-paternal.

The third trigram represents the eldest son, who seizes rule with energy and power. A solid line develops below two broken lines and presses upward forcibly. This movement is so violent that it arouses terror. It is symbolized by Thunder, which bursts forth from the earth and by its shock causes fear and trembling.

Heaven,
or the Creative

Earth,
or the Receptive

Thunder,
or the Arousing

The ancient Chinese *Book of Changes (I Ching)* powerfully demonstrates the contrast between nature, which it interprets, and symbols. The most elementary symbols are used to create an understanding of the complexity of nature. In this explanation of the *I Ching*, the designer has created a continuum from abstract to iconic to concrete to more literal.

The fourth trigram means "a plunging in." A solid line has plunged in between two broken lines and is closed in by them like water in a ravine. This trigram is the middle son: the Receptive, Earth, has obtained the middle line of the Creative, Heaven, thus forming the middle son. As an image it represents Water, the water that comes from above and is in motion on earth in streams and rivers, giving rise to all life.

The fifth trigram represents the youngest son of Heaven and Earth. Its image is Mountain; its attribute is Keeping Still, because it keeps things quiet and controls the end and the beginning of all movement.

The sixth trigram represents the eldest daughter and symbolizes Wind; it has as its attribute gentleness, which nonetheless penetrates like the wind.

The seventh trigram represents the middle daughter and means "to cling to something," "to be conditioned," "to depend or rest on something," and "brightness." Its image is Fire. Fire has no definite form but clings to the burning object and thus is bright.

The eighth trigram represents the youngest daughter; it is symbolized by the smiling Lake, and its attribute is joyousness.

Water, or the Abysmal

Mountain, or Keeping Still

Wind, or the Gentle

Fire, or the Clinging

Lake, or the Joyous

Non-Change

Equilibrium

Disturbed Equilibrium

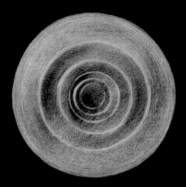

In *The Book of Changes* a distinction is made
between three kinds of change: Non-Change,
Cyclic Change, and Sequential Change.
Non-Change is the background, as it were,
against which change is made possible.
In regard to any change there must be some
ultimate fixed point, the non-changing, to
which the change can refer; otherwise there can
be no order, and everything is dissolved in
chaotic movement.

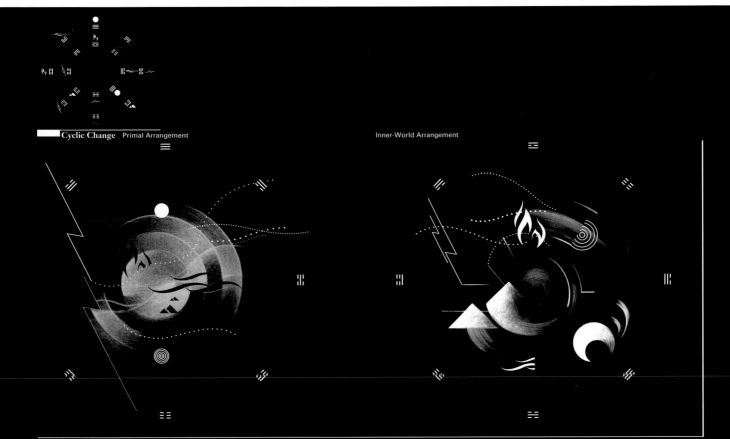

Cyclic Change Primal Arrangement

Inner-World Arrangement

Sequential Change

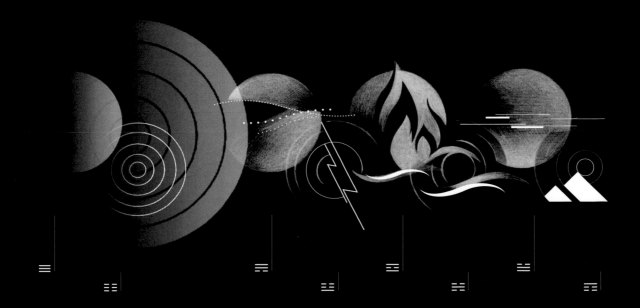

"Many will not recognize the truth of my mirror. They should realize that I'm not here to mirror the surface (photography does that better) but to penetrate it. I mirror the interior down to the heart. . . . My paintings of faces are truer than the real ones."

—Paul Klee

Abstraction and Meaning

The diagram on the facing page describes a progression from literal representation of natural form toward increasingly figurative form. By "figurative" I mean representation by a figure or a resemblance that is more symbolic, emblematic, or metaphorical.

The underlying assumption of this diagram is that our achievement as humans is less the imitation of nature and more the construction of meaning. In this view, human thought processes are to a greater or smaller degree an abstraction from nature. As such they derive from, are rooted in, and stand in clear contrast to natural form. This might mean that the evolution of an abstract form begins with a literal representation. In a culture such as ours, based on empirical seeing, this is a valid and common way to proceed in creating visual form.

Recognition of a form is only the first step toward the conveying of meaning. A literal, let's say photographic or even virtual, representation may in fact be merely superficially connected to an intended meaning. By superficial I mean consisting only of effects or simulation that excite by the illusion achieved, meaning nothing beyond this transitory excitement. Processing a form, deciphering it, is the second step.

Because meaning is cultural and not universal—even though there may be a more universal underlying formal language—literal descriptions may at first seem more appropriate in cross-cultural situations. But missing in literalness is the abstracted relation of contrast that is essential for communication and that employs the cognitive processes and make-up of the human brain. Consciously using contrast is what separates literal images from cultural statements.

It is interesting that literal representation is missing as a beginning step in many cultures where the practice of abstraction and symbolization is strong and the connection to nature intimate.

Examples on the following pages treat these questions in greater detail.

The Nature–Meaning Continuum

A continuum is a continuous succession, or whole, no part of which can be distinguished from neighboring parts except by breaking down the whole into key segments or levels. One level blends into another. Any level may partake to some degree of any other. For example, on the continuum shown opposite, a literal reproduction is likely also to some degree abstract, perhaps at the microlevel, where photographic grain or digitization or brush strokes use an artificial structure to present reality. (Remember that the reproduction is a representation.) At the other extreme, an icon or abstraction must identify recognizable key features of the real or literal to be effective.

Each level on the continuum is useful in different ways. The diagram shows how different meaning levels might "peak" at different places while retaining qualities of the other levels. (The icons on pages 52–53 are examples of images that refer recognizably to their source objects, some of which are natural forms, but on which a strong demand for clarity of abstract, rhythmic language is placed. They partake of aspects of the literal as well as the abstract in order to achieve their appropriate form.)

In the exploration shown on the following pages, figurative images of the cecropia moth exemplify the nature–meaning continuum. Within the figurative realm, the examples range from concrete to iconic to abstract.

These studies are designed to facilitate learning to locate an image's characteristic relative to its functional purposes and to provide a conceptual framework for modifying images to better serve their functions.

The Symbolic Meaning of an Image

Any image or object has potential symbolic meaning for a given audience. There is no *inherent* reason for anyone to agree on its meaning. It acquires symbolic meaning.

Yet images constructed with a strong abstract structure based on contrast carry with them a greater inherent power to be seen as symbols. In general this means that unnecessary information is eliminated in order to clarify a form for communication. "Leaving out" can be both more interesting and clearer than "showing all."

Abstraction can derive from nature in an authentic way, retaining the essential qualities of organic relationship and inventiveness true to nature. Conversely, caricatured, decorative, and imitative images are alienations from natural sources, lying outside the path of connection to nature. The range of possible expression widens as the movement toward abstraction increases. (Nature *itself* cannot be shown, because any image of nature is a representation.)

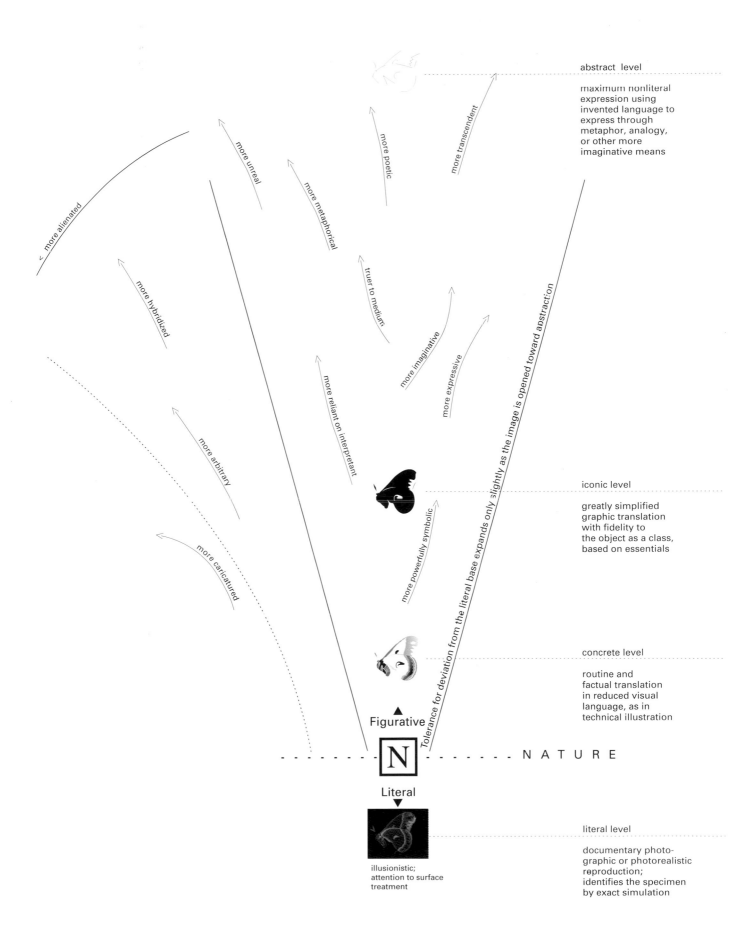

abstract level

maximum nonliteral
expression using
invented language to
express through
metaphor, analogy,
or other more
imaginative means

more transcendent

more poetic

more unreal

more metaphorical

more alienated

truer to medium

more hybridized

more imaginative

more expressive

Tolerance for deviation from the literal base expands only slightly as the image is opened toward abstraction

more reliant on interpretant

more arbitrary

more powerfully symbolic

iconic level

greatly simplified
graphic translation
with fidelity to
the object as a class,
based on essentials

more caricatured

concrete level

routine and
factual translation
in reduced visual
language, as in
technical illustration

Figurative
▲

N

Literal
▼

- - - - - - - - - - - - - - - - - N A T U R E

illusionistic;
attention to surface
treatment

literal level

documentary photo-
graphic or photorealistic
reproduction;
identifies the specimen
by exact simulation

Background: Why the cecropia moth?
This specimen has long been in plain view
in my house; I have passed it daily
for many years. The choice to use it as
a base for these studies was not wholly
arbitrary: its markings tend toward
the abstract, and its size is convenient
for both scanning and drawing. I was
well into the translations before I
discovered that as a moth, the cecropia
didn't have much of a life: it ate
nothing, emerging for a brief nocturnal existence from its cocoon to lay its
eggs and die.

*Studies in progressive abstraction from a
natural form*

Goals:
—*to improve observational skills*
—*to deepen a connection to nature as a
source*
—*to explore ways to retain meanings
and qualities of a natural form while
translating it into a graphic language*
—*to establish a new correlation of parts
to create an organic whole*
—*to retain a sense of the dynamic values
of nature:*
structural
metamorphic
climactic
stratified
organic
diverse
adaptive
mysterious
—*to become aware of how form can be
pushed to extremes of expressive
abstraction when progressively and credi-
bly derived from the natural source*

Process:
1.
*worry-free, unself-conscious, crude
sketching to create fast, intuitive, natural
responses to form*
2.
*more conscious moves toward controlled
form-making*
3.
*translation in black and white with vary-
ing degrees of abstraction*
4.
introduction of color
5.
*sampling of subsets for heightened,
effective abstraction*
6.
*derivation with stylistic overtones
(Mayan)*
7.
*expansion phase: experiments with
hybrid forms and the opening of new
directions for dramatization of
specific qualities and further formal
invention*

■
An expression of
lightness, tentative-
ness, and crude
fluttering emanates
from the worry-free
sketching process.

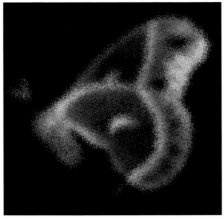

■ Drawing with crude means helps identify essential qualities. The blurred version (above) does this overall; the sketches seek differentiation based on selected information.

■
Here the relative pro-
portions of the object
are more precisely
sought. Though the
intent is accurate
description, the result-
ing velocity of the
strokes and the
overlay of seek lines
and edge definition
take on an expressive
character of energy
and flight.

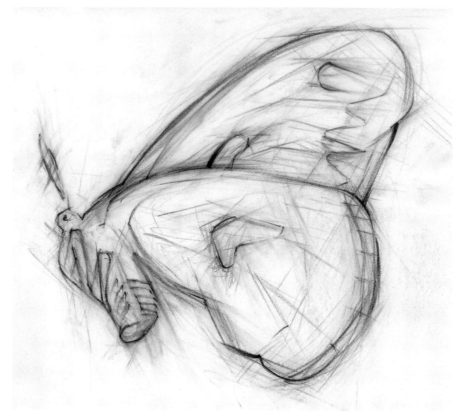

■
The experience of
mapping out the
whole object, above,
prepares the way
for a reduction in the
number of lines
used to abstract the
object.

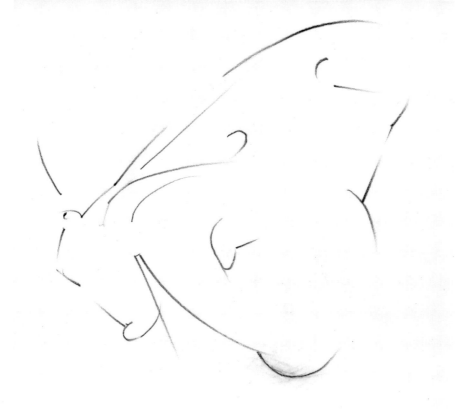

■
Further linear simplification and tonal representation of a few larger elements, done first as separate studies, are combined in the image at right. The crayon stroke recalls the feathery surface structure of the moth without losing its identity as medium. These are moves toward formulating basic contrast ideas: dot to line, dot and line to tonalities.

■
Reinterpretation as a simplified, sharply defined shape with minimal detail to express essential qualities.

■·
Progressive abstraction:
The image is trans-
lated into languages of
pure form—dot,
line, shape—released
as pure rhythm in
simplest possible
terms. Each has its
own formal constructs,
adhering to the
original shape of the
source object.

■
Here liberties are taken to use the object as a means for metaphorical representation. The wings become faces, looking to the ground (from which the moth has sprung) and to the sky (in which it now freely floats). The antennae are exaggerated as sensors. Forms become symbolically meaningful when meaning is assigned. A poetic congruity to the natural form is retained.

■ Translation with
concrete formal
resolution and color
derived from the
original object.
Abstraction is present
but is subordinate to
the more ordinary
total image.

■ The sifts of parts on
the facing page show
how "mothness" can
be conveyed more
inventively by using
less of the image.

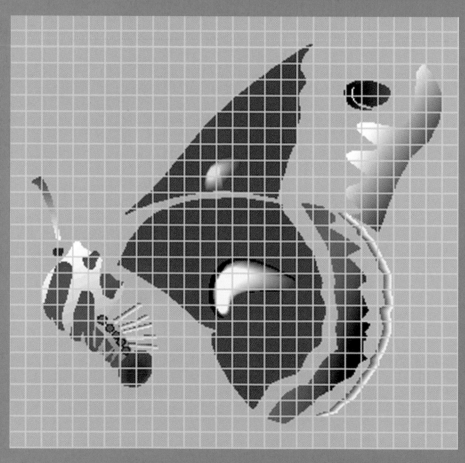

■ Although this image
was not drawn on a
grid, placing it on this
artificial device pro-
vides a measure for
the degree of abstrac-
tion attained in the
drawing. Grid and
drawing tend to mesh
as one image.

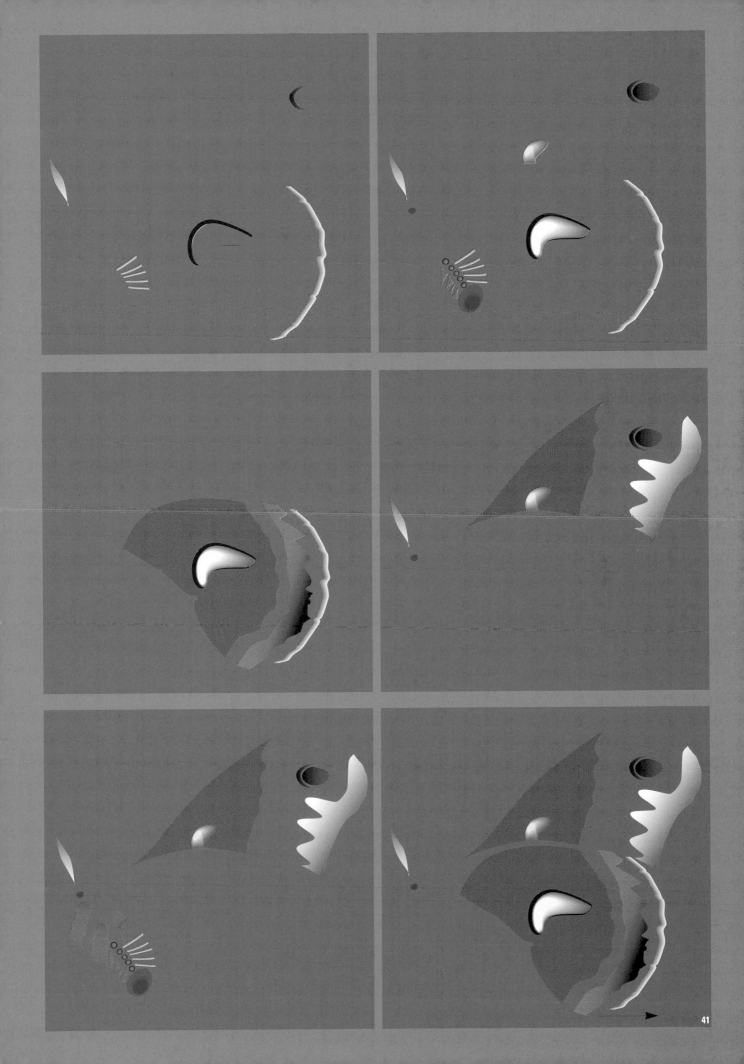

Distortion is another
method of abstraction.
Here the translation
shown on page 40
successively dissolves
into images that can
signify aspects of
the object: fluttering,
metamorphosis,
dissolution.

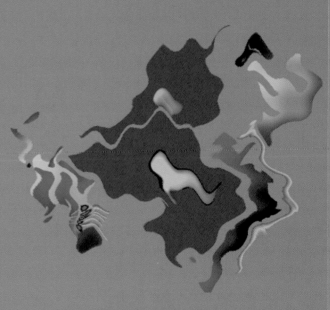

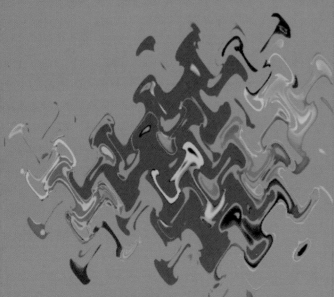

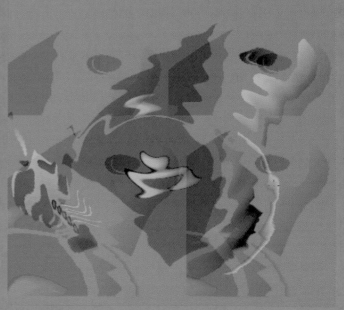

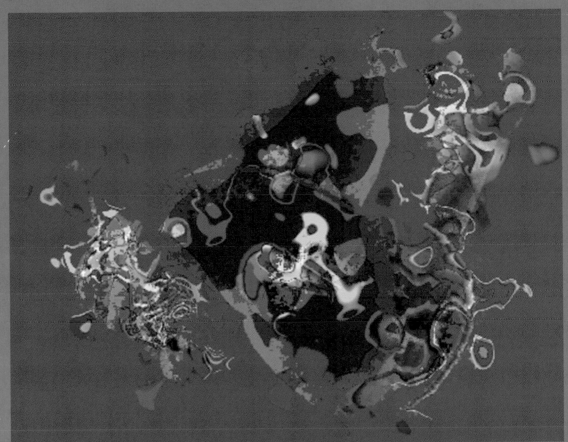

The ultimate disinte-
gration of the image
carries within it
myriad forms and
tumultuous color for
imaginative interpreta-
tion. The image still
"flies" but prefigures
its entire metamorphic
existence.

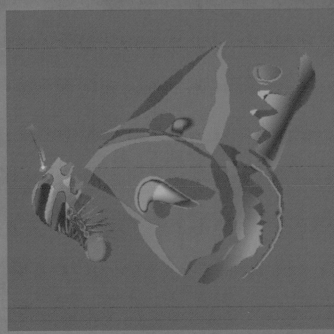

The carefree, colorful
version at the right
becomes a butterfly
instead of a moth, a
flower visitor, denying
its nocturnal existence
and sober color.
The image is alienated
from the trajectory
proceeding from
the source (like a horse
with zebra stripes).

■ This translation is a convergence using as sources the natural object and Mayan stylistic means—of which the stone carving above is an example. Belonging both to nature and to a viewpoint, the image partakes of two worlds—the natural and the invented.

■ Color adds to the sense of mystery and cosmic significance while corresponding in general palette to the original object.

■ Testing sifts of the parts, at right, shows again the power of abstraction to excite the imagination.

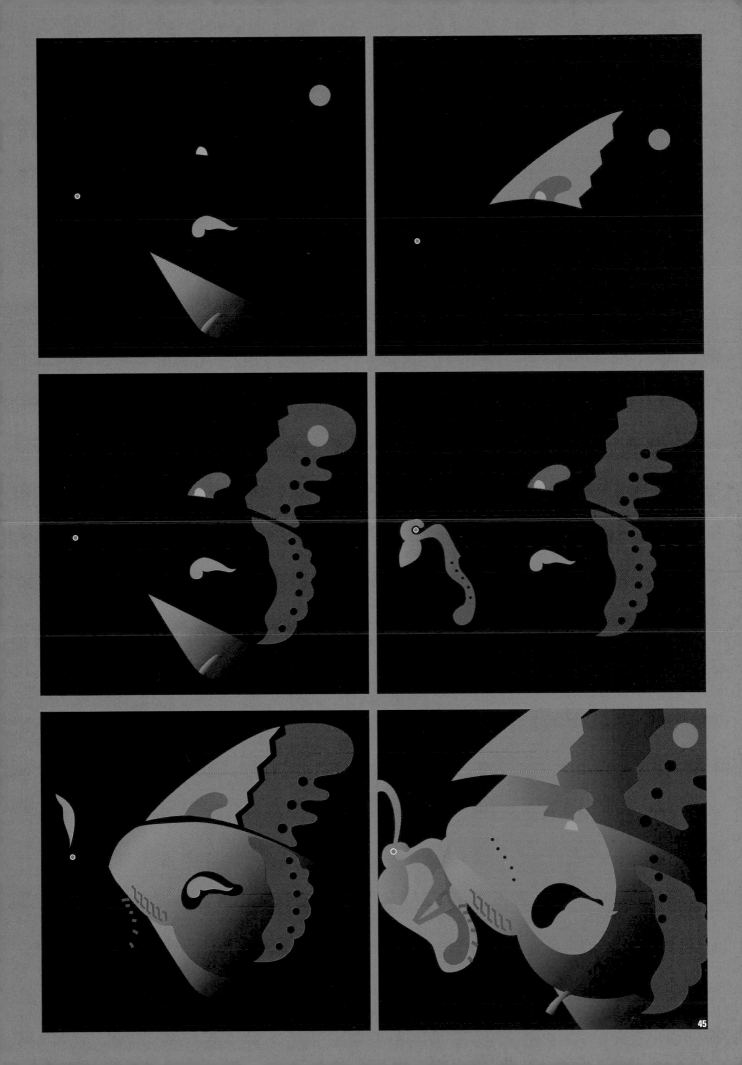

Hybrids are formed
either by recombining
different translation
languages or
by overlaying new
elements.

Hybrids are potentially
of great visual
interest, but alienation
from the natural
source tends to make
them more whimsical
and ephemeral.

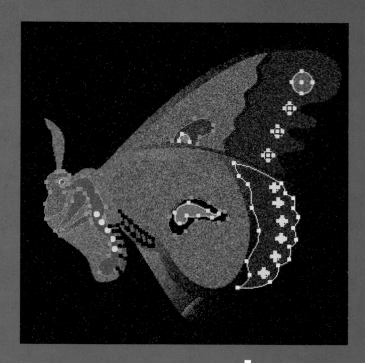

Seeing elements
leaping out as bright
lights is akin to the
garish overlay of lights
and glittering reflec-
tive materials on more
subdued votive arti-
facts in Mesoamerican
cultures.

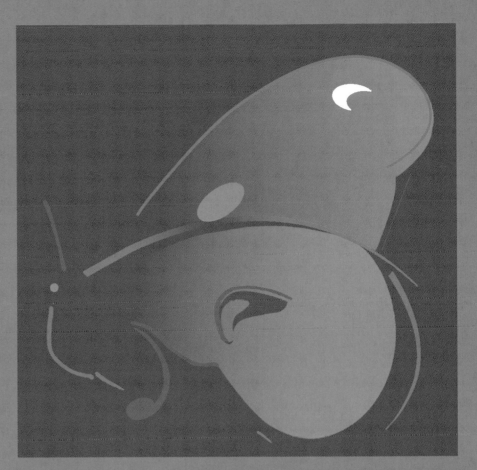

■ Hybridized color
in an imposed warm-
cool contrast.

■ Fusion with a back-
ground creates a
formal hybrid of line
and texture.

47

■
Hybrids combining
vestiges of the natural-
istic form and abstract
translations are
not only the source of
visual interest—
like ruins—but the
basis for drawings that
isolate detail in
a larger framework.

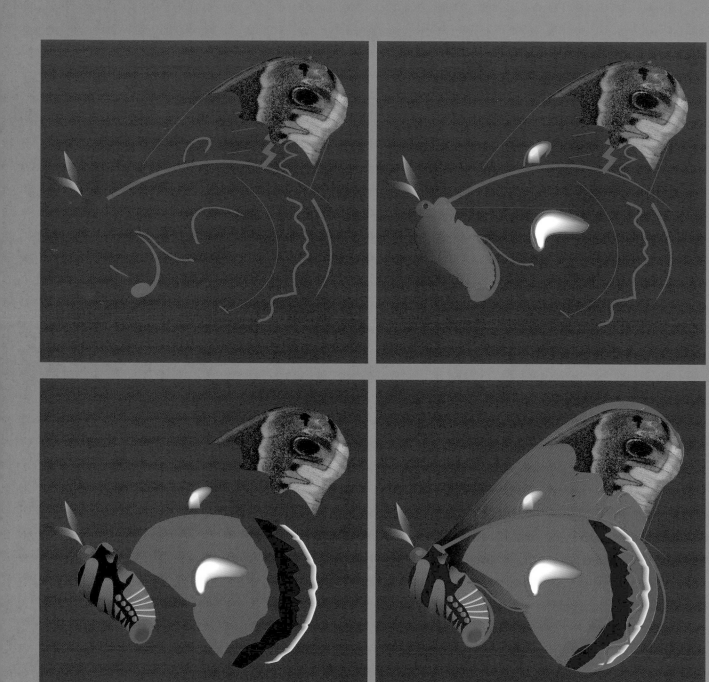

Drawing from . . .

Transformational Programs

Programs for transforming images are text-based. They use verbally stated concepts as beginning points for thinking about visual form and creating meaning.

In this chapter we first build a visual icon reduced to its essential qualities. This icon is then subjected to a set of verbally stated transformations. The variations and combinations produced create new visual contexts for the icon and qualify its meaning.

As we develop the visual transformation series, we research a concept for relating a text to the images. The subsequent coupling of image and text either underscores the visual sense of the image or redirects its meaning in the coupling, often with unexpected quality.

Phases of a Transformational Program

We begin by developing a visual icon largely from memory according to a few given parameters. This icon is a concrete, denotative image.

The icon forms a base for a series of operations to extend its meaning. The resulting constructs and comparisons are formal responses to a program of changes. This phase is increasingly connotative—that is, meanings are inferred by the way the icon is changed or combined with other image materials. The images in this phase are largely wordless, allowing the mind to find meaning in visual connections.

In a third phase, we research a concept for relating a text to the images. The subsequent coupling of image and text is a transformation that produces a new level of intended meaning. Whereas the preceding phase tends to yield images of direct meaning—in the spirit of the icon—the coupling with texts produces a new layer of metaphorical and connotative meaning. This sequence of phases (which is inverted from most problem-solving approaches) is valuable because of the early effort expended to make the images speak without the support of words. In this way we create a strong visual presence that does not diminish to a background status when combined with words. When word and image are uniquely integrated, visual form transcends mere ambiance.

Words, then, function at three points in this process:

1. at the beginning to define the criteria for the visual quality of the icon;

2. then to provide the stimulus for a generic set of variations, applicable to any icon; and

3. last when a "story" develops and text is added for greater precision of meaning.

The result is a system of signs—verbal and visual—that work together to generate a viewpoint. The significance of this project is discovering that viewpoint varies with context and that contexts can be invented. It is about creating meaning and about using contextual relevance to achieve that goal.

Icons and Icon Quality

Computer interfaces, which use iconic images, have brought the word *icon* into common parlance. From this we have grasped the idea that an icon bears an immediate likeness to the thing it represents: the closer the likeness, the better the icon. The need for icons to resemble what they represent imposes on them a certain ordinary quality, making them almost inherently predictable. The element of common recognition is precisely what is useful. As the range of transformations, combinations, and associations emerges, the persistent recognition of the base form—preserving its home identity, mundane as this may be at the outset—is crucial as the icon assumes new roles. Thus an alarm clock can be the catalyst icon to discuss positive and negative ideas about progress or a syringe can be the stimulus to create searing commentary on drug addiction. Symbolic and metaphoric functions are outgrowths of an extended encounter with the icon and its domains.

And even though the icon may be prosaic in content, there are ways to bring it to an essentially rhythmic state with a strong abstract quality. A sampling of icons with this quality is shown on the following two pages. We strive for a simplicity akin to that of a classic letter form.

A typical dilemma designers face is that our topics may be light and their form inherently linear, whereas a more massive form would admit a greater range of transformations. This is because a bold image, like a bold letter form, can function both in juxtaposition to other forms and as a mask for other forms. With lightness—the sense of forms taking flight—as an expressive ideal and massiveness as the pragmatic goal, the quality sought is a tension between the two in which massive form is counteracted by fineness in the detail. Some inherently linear image topics, like needle and thread, resist any effort to create mass and have to be dealt with in their own terms.

< icon >

literal	concrete	abstract

The icon hovers between the concrete and the abstract, sharing recognizability with the concrete and rhythmic form with the abstract.

*and they remain criteria while visual form—
multi-planed, unpredictable, colorful, spatial—
stretches the sense and plays out
the effective meaning.*

Defining the Icon and Its Domains

In brainstorming an icon subject, it is not hard to generate long
lists of word associations. We distinguish between those
that effectively describe the icon and those that are generally
not helpful in appraising the rightness of the form. Using
the hand as an example, we need only a few good descriptors
with strong visual equivalence to help establish the form:

verbs:	*adjectives:*	*nouns:*
extend	firm	palm
reach	organic	fingers
	curvilinear	knuckles

More words would be too much information at this phase.
Fussy detail would interfere with the potential for adding
counterform, including additional detail, as one of the
transforming options. Think of the icon as a simple, memo-
rable melody.

As we know, the hand relates to myriad other topics, whether
hand signals (and hence communication), hand tools,
hand crafts, hand anatomy (in detail), hand tricks, and handwriting. There is a world of gloves and rings and nails
(and through this, fashion and fads). There are worlds of
sports and medicine and gardening, to say nothing of
literature, philosophy, and religion. By such association, the
hand opens its many domains to us for further inquiry.

In the example on page 60, the hand is associated with the verb
adorn. The quotation linked with this image is: "For
loveliness needs not the foreign aid of ornament, but is when
unadorned adorned the most," by James Thomson. The
relation between the tendency toward excess and the reverse
tendency toward the bare essential becomes the thought-
provoking totality of the expression. The domains of the
immediate and the philosophical are brought into effective
proximity. This tension is the conceptual viewpoint for
the coupling of texts throughout the hand series.

Warm-Up for an Independent Project

This project was conceived as a warm-up to be done while
students develop an idea for an independent senior project.
It offers a review of many aspects of basic design while
honing verbal and conceptual skills. As can be seen by the
excerpts presented, the level of complexity and sophistication varies according to the student and the topic.

Design Process:

1.
Define icon as compared to symbol,
cliché, and archetype.

2.
Sketch icons that are key to your topic
area. First sketch an iconic image of the
given object from memory, attempting to
represent the object in its essence.
The goal is the greatest possible simplicity, unquestionable recognition, and
good positive and negative form.
The image should be devoid of distracting
stylistic mannerisms or eccentric overtones. Use a pencil or brush and ink in
a 4"x 4" format for first sketches, in black
and white only. Do not use templates
or rulers. Make fast multiple versions to
compare before focusing on one.

3.
Compile a key word set (verbs, adjectives,
nouns) to function as criteria for the icon
image.

4.
Refine the visual quality of the icon, building on your skills in drawing, letter forms,
design systems, and communications.
Test your icon against the form of real
objects. Your drawing will be discussed in
a group session for feedback. Your final
black-and-white line drawing must fit
within an 8" square. A version drawn on
the computer will be required for subsequent phases.

5.
Transform the icon, adjusting it if necessary. After you have sketched the first
variations, correct newly revealed defects
in the icon.

6.
Begin a search for texts related to your
topic area.

7.
Develop a format to present the icon and
its variants using the following guidelines:
  a. an external format of 8.5" x 11".
  b. an internal format of a 6" square to
be placed and marked in a unique way
derived from or contrasting with the
icon's visual character.
  c. "home" location of icon in internal
format. ("Home" is a default location
upon which to build.)
  d. "home" location and typographic
character of text messages.

8.
Experiment with dynamic coupling of
texts and visual variations in the format.

9.
Edit your studies to satisfy these criteria:
meaning, interest, formal structure, and
sequential rhythm. In your final series,
use only those studies that contribute to
your series concept.

10.
Bring the series to a consistently high
craft level.

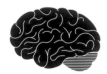

Icons are arranged
alphabetically across
these two pages.
Are more clues
needed to confirm
their identities?

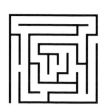

Sample base image:

The Program of Transformations

Category A:
formal changes to the icon

A.1 Deconstruction as a function of the image. (The hand is segmented at the knuckles.)

A.2 Deconstruction as a chance operation. (Crumpled paper produces an overall wrinkling.)

A.3 A curvilinear version if icon is primarily rectilinear, or vice versa. (Angular form mechanizes the form.)

A.4 Transformation of a part: distortion, scale change, rectilinear to curvilinear, inversion, etc. (Crossing the fingers creates a signal change.)

A.5 Maximum cropping possible to maintain recognition.

A.6 Repetition:
a. —ornamental (the effect is primarily decorative).
b. —amplified (the effect is dramatized).
c. —random (the effect invites questioning).

A.7 Dimensional depth shown in two dimensions. (Drawing volume is only one way of expressing depth.)

A.8 A three-dimensional version. (In this case the folder containing the whole series employs a dimensional shift by breaking image components into separate planes.)

A.9 Color conversion. (A color shift from gray in the heel of the hand to red at the finger tips extends the reach outward. The actual color is shown on the cover for this book.)

A.1

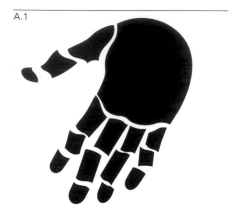

A.2

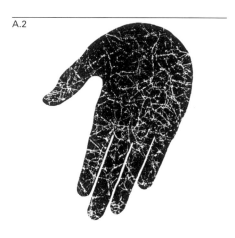

A.3

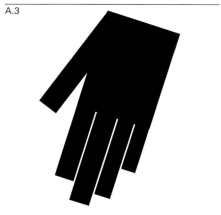

A.4

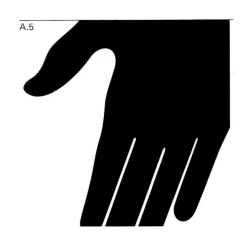
A.5

A.6.a

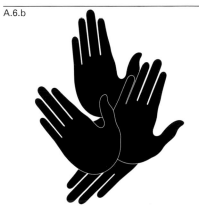
A.6.b

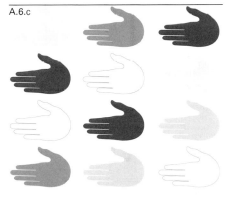
A.6.c

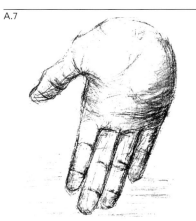
A.7

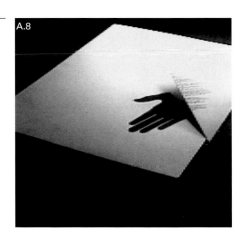
A.8

A.9

55

Category B:
icon influenced by something else

B.1 Influenced by music. (See chapter 3, Drawing from Music, for extensive detail on this aspect.)

B.2 Transformed to reflect the meaning of an applied action word.

Category C:
icon combined with something else

C.1 Combined with an actual object representation (photo or rubbing).

C.2 Combined with the letter form that most clearly represents the icon. (H for hand is the obvious choice.)

C.3 Combined with your own hand or face form, functionally meaningful. (Clapping is the function evoked.)

C.4 Combined with your own hand or face form, formally related. (No specific meaning is intended in the combination; the image is aesthetically based, using similarity and contrast. It should feel meaningful.)

C.5 Combined with another icon (trade with any classmate) to create a meaning in the combination. (The combination with a butterfly icon imparts a sense of release rather than capture.)

C.6 Combined with a related texture to amplify a meaning. (This texture evokes the sense of a bandage.)

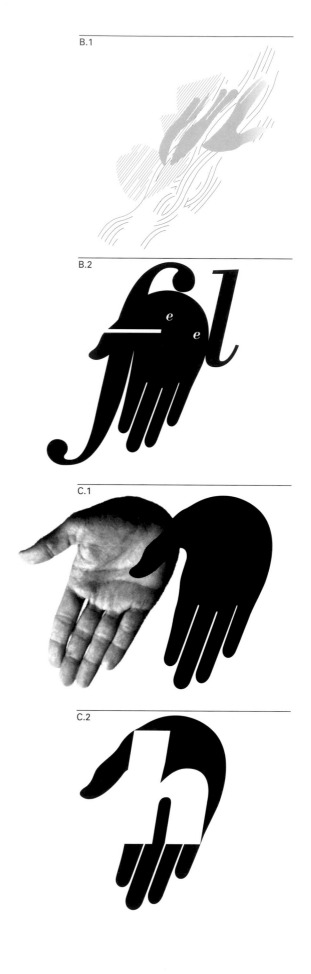

B.1

B.2

C.1

C.2

C.3

C.4

C.5

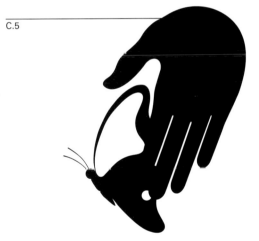

C.6

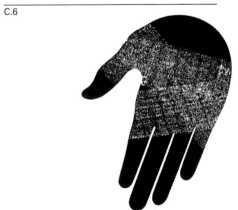

C.7   Combined with three images related in form and function:

a.   —the image relates to the icon in both form and function. (A different hand icon is added.)

b.   —the image relates in form but contrasts in function. (The leaf is similar to the hand in its extension from a rounded base. It contrasts in function as a vegetative compared to a human form.)

c.   —the image relates in function but contrasts in form. (The gift package relates to the giving gesture of the hand but contrasts in its soft, blocky form. Although the loops of the bow relate to the fingers, the overall effect is one of formal contrast. Every relation is the composite of *both* similar and contrasting features.)

C.8   Placed in another time or culture. (The hand as religious gesture from a historic Christian image is scaled to the hand to effect a relation between new and old.)

C.9   Integrated with a word or number. (Mathematic functions are suggested.)

C.10 Augmented to alter the connotation. (The addition of nails and a ring has a radical effect.)

C.11 A free collage reflecting use of the icon. (The collage is informed by reference to the work of Kurt Schwitters.)

Category D:
icon as a metaphor for something else

D.1   As a metaphor for a human body part: combined with analogous or contrasting other parts. Because the hand icon is itself a body part, the student has used it as a fig leaf surrogate against a human torso. An interesting example from another series based on a feathered headdress suggests a dancer through slight augmentation and radical change of orientation:

Category E:
other expansions

E.1   A kinetic sequence. (A kinetic event can take place in one frame or in multiple frames.)

E.2   The icon as a base for a path or diagram showing information related to it.

E.3   Optional other version(s) discovered in the process. (Usually these take the form of combinations of previous transformations. The example combines A.4, transformation of a part, with a mathematic structure.)

C.7.a
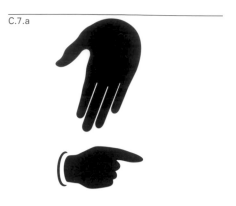

C.7.b

C.7.c
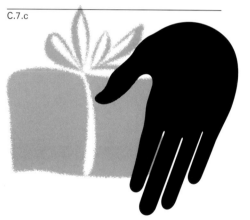

C.8

C.9

C.10

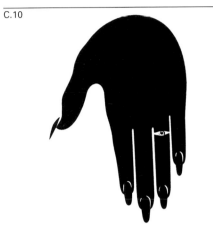

C.11

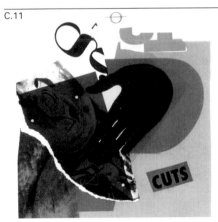

D.1

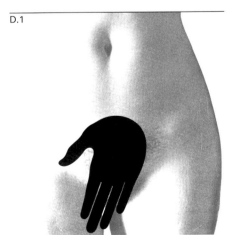

E.1

h e l l o !

E.2

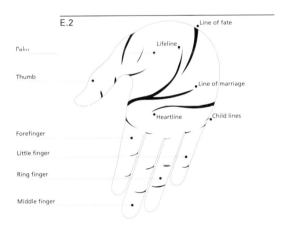

Palm

Thumb

Forefinger

Little finger

Ring finger

Middle finger

Line of fate

Lifeline

Line of marriage

Heartline

Child lines

E.3

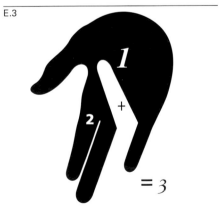

Specific text and
image elements are
shown here in their
"home" locations.
Tension is established
in the visual image
transformation and
confirmed by the
accompanying verb.
A new level of tension
comes from reading
the text.

For loveliness
needs not
the foreign
aid of
ornament,
but is when
unadorned
adorned
the most.

— *James Thomson*

4

adorn

•••

Art is a human
activity, consisting
in this, that one
man consciously,
by means of
external signs,
hands on to
others feelings he
has worked
through, and
other people
are infected by
these feelings
and also
experience them.

— *Leo Tolstoy*

touch

...

Examples of how letter and icon combinations, created abstractly as transformation exercises, gain other meanings in combination with other text.

h   The letter h forms a unity with the hand using scale and shape similarity and effectively using negative form. Offering is in tension with withholding.

R   The road icon is in an effective scale relation to the letter R, joining to create an image that gives a sense of lift beyond the confines of the road, as the poem by Robert Frost suggests.

jump   The contrast of the separated letters against the blur of the slurred icon expresses the suddenness and evasiveness of the action.

L   The script L, which stands in an obvious formal congruence with the lizard, transcends its normal syrupy quality to symbolize a sharply competitive relationship.

c   As a symbol for passing time, the combination of the letter c and the candle harks back to the pictographic origins of the alphabet in a modern way. The series celebrates birthdays.

fear   By scale inversion the snake is rendered harmless—a protector—and fear is accentuated by color, size, and constriction.

The road at the top of the rise
Seems to come to an end
And take off into the skies.
So at the distant bend.

It seems to go into a wood,
The place of standing still
As long the trees have stood.
But say what Fancy will.

The mineral drops that explode
To drive my ton of car
Are limited to the road.
They deal with near and far.

But have almost nothing to do
With the absolute flight and rest
The universal blue
And local green suggest.

**The Middleness
of the Road**

by
Robert Frost

18

... 5

3 . 8 . 1835

*The characters of
our alphabet were originally
pictures or symbols of
which lettering now stops short.*

Frederic Goudy

17

In Japan.........................I remember...................

.........my mother always told me...............

there was always a white snake in the house......

..Protecting.

: 17

Examples of how collages, created abstractly as
transformation exercises, gain other meanings
in combination with text.

The example below shows a collage in its
"pure" state without the addition of text.

Man unites
himself with
the world
in the process
of creation.

— *Erich Fromm*

18

join

"[The labyrinth] is...at once the cosmos, the world,

the individual life, the temple, the town,

the man, the womb—*die Urmutter—auf die Mutter (earth)*,

the convolutions of the brain, the consciousness,
the heart,

the pilgrimmage, the journey, and the Way."

—Jill Purce: *The Mystic Spiral*

23

• In the past, man has looked to the bear as a teacher, observing how it lives and dwells with nature in harmony.

beauty is in the eye of the beholder. What one person considers ugly may seem beautiful to another. The idea is very old and was stated in various ways from the sixteenth century on. Shakespeare's version is close to the modern; "beauty is bought by judgment of the eye" (Love's Labour's Lost, 2:1). Possibly the first exact statement of the cliche in print was in Margaret Hungerford's Molly Baun (1878).

What makes

beautiful

30

Teacher Text by George Pleska 19

Is but a dim-remembered story
Of the old time entombed

Runs

There is no need
to read into
it...the desert
r e v e a l s
itself and its
creatures to
those who walk
among them.

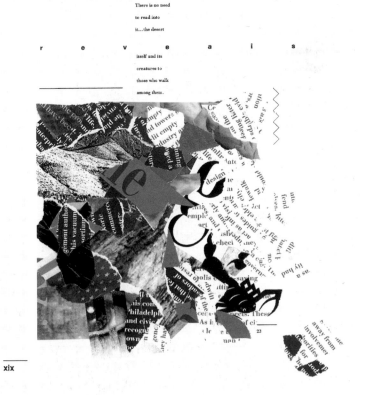

23

xix

Icon base: snake

Series concept:
Texts derived from other students' responses
to the question "What do you think of snakes?"
In the excerpts shown, the meanings of
the visual transformations can vary from a
reference to the snake's physiology in no. 28
to internal doubt in no. 33. In relation to
content, the sequence is random. The icon
maintains a constant size and home position to
emphasize differences in form.

Typographic concept:
Exaggerated ellipses linking phrases to suggest
snaking.

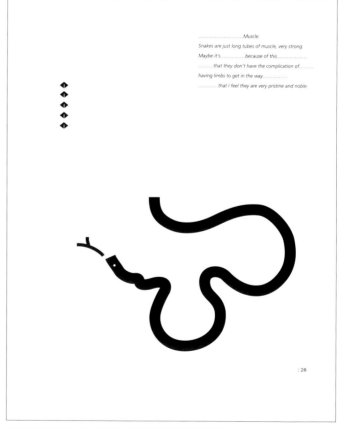

My first image is..................that of a snake
..................smoothly slithering..........
............along the ground ....
..................sneaking up on someone
............unsuspectingly..................

: 1

B.2 combined with action word ▲

..........................Muscle.
Snakes are just long tubes of muscle, very strong.
Maybe it's.............because of this................
..........that they don't have the complication of........
having limbs to get in the way...............
............that I feel they are very pristine and noble.

: 28

E.3 other: monoline conversion ▲

..................Sometimes.....................
Severe thunderstorms.....................
...freak me a bit

: 9

A.3 rectilinear conversion ▲

I don't care for worms..................slugs.........
no rational reason...............they just give me the creeps.

: 18

C.7.c related function/contrasting form ▲

What do I fear..........................more than snakes?
..........At times............ I fear that............
...I won't be able to..............
......live energetically enough............before I die
That my life won't be.............................
.............................spiritually stimulating enough.

: 33

A.4 distortion of a part ▲

A loss of control.............................
..........in any number of situations.................
is what I fear............more than snakes

: 35

A.2 deconstruction as chance ▲

Icon base: fairy

Series concept:
Texts are derived from diverse literary sources.
There is no specific order to the sequence. The
icon maintains a constant size and fairly
consistent home position. The special problem
is to create overall a sense of lightness and
small size using a stark black and white form.

Typographic concept:
The orientation of flush left, line-for-line
typography to the right angle element is
abstractly analogous to the relation between
body and wings in the fairy image.

Every time a child says "I don't believe in
fairies" there is a little fairy somewhere

— J.M.Barrie

B.1 deconstruction/function ▲

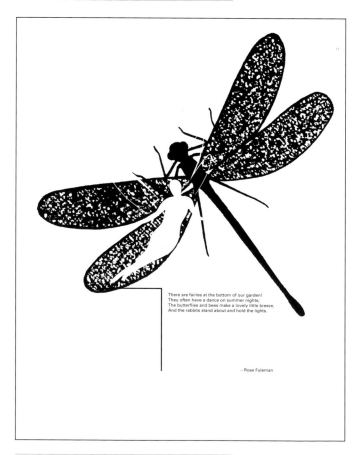

There are fairies at the bottom of our garden!
They often have a dance on summer nights;
The butterflies and bees make a lovely little breeze,
And the rabbits stand about and hold the lights.

— Rose Fyleman

C.7.a related form/related function (flight) ▲

Believe me, if all those endearing young charms,
Which I gaze on so fondly today,
Were to change by tomorrow, and fleet in my arms,
Like fairy gifts fading away!

– Thomas Moore

A.2 deconstruction as chance ▲

There are fairies at the bottom of our garden!
It's not so very, very far away,
You pass the gardener's shed and you just keep straight ahead–
I do so hope they've really come to stay.
There's a little wood, with moss in it and beetles,
And a little stream that quietly runs through;
You wouldn't think they'd dare to come merrymaking there–
Well, they do.

– Rose Fyleman

C.7.b related form/contrasting function ▲

Don't go looking for fairies.
They'll fly away if you do.
You never can see the fairies
Till they come looking for you.

– Eleanor Farjeon

C.3 combined with hand/functional ▲

Have you seen the fairies dancing in the air,
And dashing off behind the stars to tidy up their hair?
I have, I have; I've been there!

– Rose Fyleman

C.8 placed in another time or culture ▲

Icon base: pen

Series concept:
Texts are first lines of novels.

Typographic concept:
The type maintains a bookish quality that is
helped by the use of an enlarged initial letter.

When he was really thirteen, my brother Jem got his arm badly broken at the elbow.
— *To Kill A Mockingbird by Harper Lee*

A.2 deconstruction as chance ▲

Kino awakened in the near dark.
— *The Pearl by John Steinbeck*

A.7 dimensional depth ▲

"To the man who loves art for its own sake," remarked Sherlock
Holmes, tossing aside the advertisement sheet of the *Daily Telegraph*,
"it is frequently in its least important and lowliest manifestations
that the keenest pleasure is to be derived."
— *The Adventure of the Copper Beeches* by Sir Arthur Conan Doyle

C.6 combined with related texture ▲

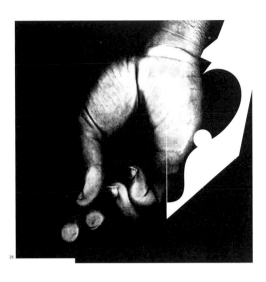

Squire Trelawney, Dr. Livesey, and the rest of these gentlemen
having asked me to write down the whole particulars about Treasure
Island, from the beginning to the end, keeping nothing back but
the bearings of the island, and that only because there is still treasure
not yet lifted, I take up my pen in the year of grace 1759 and go back
to the time when my father kept the Admiral Benbow Inn and the
brown old seaman with the sabre cut first took up his lodging under
our roof.
— *Treasure Island* by Robert Louis Stevenson

C.4 with hand/formal ▲

For the first fifteen years of our lives, Danny and I lived within five
blocks of each other and neither of us knew of the other's existence.
— *The Chosen* by Chaim Potik

C.1 combined with actual object ▲

In my younger and more vulnerable years, my father gave me some
advice that I've been turning over in my mind ever since.
— *The Great Gatsby* by F. Scott Fitzgerald

C.4 combined with face/formal ▲

Icon base: road

Series concept:
Texts are poems related to the road theme by various authors. For example, the two levels of the A.7 dimensional depth treatment show staying and going as foreground and background, respectively. The icon varies radically in size and position.

Typographic concept:
Line-for-line treatment respecting authors' style.

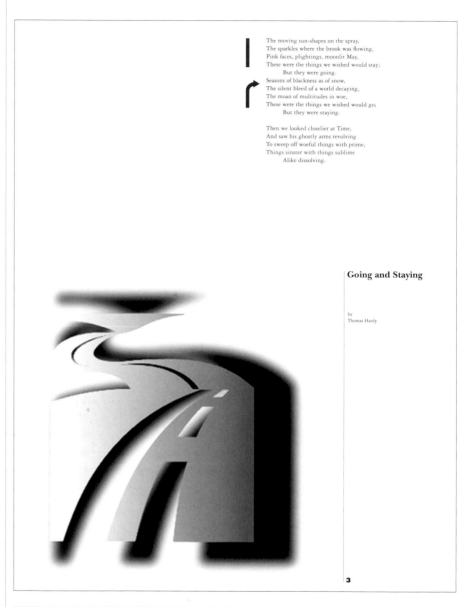

The moving sun-shapes on the spray,
The sparkles where the brook was flowing,
Pink faces, plightings, moonlit May,
These were the things we wished would stay;
　　　But they were going.
Seasons of blackness as of snow,
The silent bleed of a world decaying,
The moan of multitudes in woe,
These were the things we wished would go;
　　　But they were staying.

Then we looked closelier at Time,
And saw his ghostly arms revolving
To sweep off woeful things with prime,
Things sinster with things sublime
　　　Alike dissolving.

Going and Staying

by
Thomas Hardy

3

A.7 dimensional depth ▲

A.3 rectilinear version ▲

A.6.a and b repetition, ornamental and amplified ▲

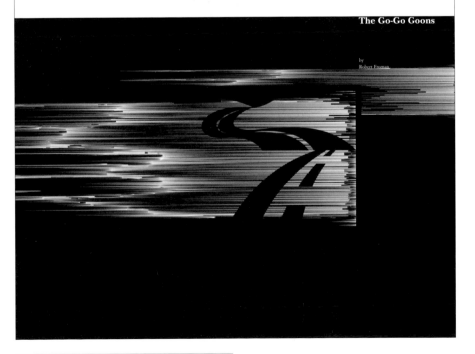

C.6 combined with related texture ▲

Nobody riding the roads today
But I hear the living rush
far away from my heart

Nobody meeting on the streets
But I rage from the crowded
overtones of emptiness

Nobody sleeping in my bed
But I breathe like windows
broken by emergencies

Nobody laughing anymore
But I see the world split
and twisted up like open stone

Nobody riding the roads today
But I hear the living rush
far away from my heart

On a Tree
Fallen A cross
the Road

by
Robert Frost

B.2 combined with action word ▲

Workers using private cars for commuting

| 0 | 25 | 50 | 75 | 100% |

Amsterdam
Hamburg
Hong Kong
Munich
Perth
Pheonix
Stockholm
Sydney
Tokyo
Toronto
Vienna
Washington

**Nobody Riding
the Roads Today**

by
J. Jordan

13

E.2 diagram ▲

" DON'T WALK."
"   "
" DON'T WALK."
"   "
" DON'T WALK."

That sign talks too much.
Makes you have to WALK.

Orders

by
Robert Froman

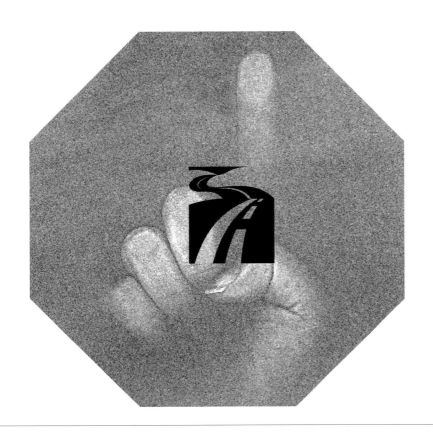

12

C.3 combined with hand/functional ▲

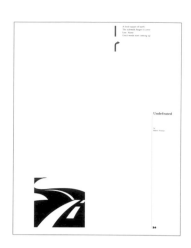

Two roads diverged in a yellow wood,
And sorry I could not travel both
And be one traveler, long I stood
And looked down one as far as I could
To where it bent in the undergrowth:

Then took the other, as just as fair,
And having perhaps the better claim,
Because it was grassy and wanted wear,
Though as for that the passing there
Had worn them really about the same,

And both that morning equally lay
In leaves no step had trodden black.
Oh, I kept the first for another day!
Yet knowing how way leads on to way,
I doubted if I should ever come back.

The Road
Not Taken

by
Robert Frost

...

And where my youth was, now the Sun in you grows hot, your
day is young, my place you take triumphantly. All along
it's been for you, for this lowering of your horns in challenge, She
had her will of me and will not
let my struggling spirit in itself be free.

Rites of Passage

by
Robert Duncan

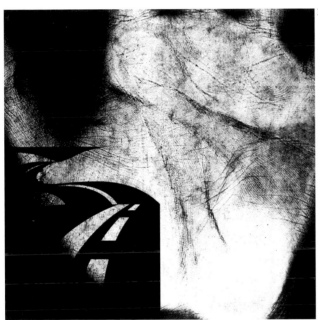

2

C.4 combined with hand/formal ▲

C.7.b related form/contrasting function ▼

Wind, Clouds, and the delicate curve of the world
Stretching so far away....
On a cloud in the clear sight of heaven
Sit Kali and Jesus, disputing.
Tree shadows, cloud shadows
Falling across the body of the world
That sleeps with one arm thrown across her eyes....
A wind stirs in the daisies
And trees are singing,
"These houses and these gardens are illusions."
Leaf shadows, cloud shadows,
And the wind moving as far as the eye can reach....

Wind, Clouds, and
the Delicate Curve
of the World

by
Robert Bly

23

Flying from the dry pall of the city
I watched road wrinkle   dwindle up the dune range
& disappear in the general pox
of eucalyptus   the skin of a land
hard & vacant as the faces
of swagmen in Australian painting

But suddenly all is tressed
with turbulence
violet smoke rocketing up & away to the Tasman—
Fire is loose   wild in a hundred hills
& the gray woods exploding

…

**The Gray Woods
Exploding**

by
Earl Birney

7

E.3 other: contrasting form and function ▲

C.10 augmented ▲

C.7.b related form/contrasting function ▲

C.5 combined with another icon (footprint) ▲

Icon base: syringe

Series concept:
"A Cry from Hell," texts excerpted from *Naked Lunch*, chronicles of a drug addict by William S. Burroughs.

Typographic concept:
To dramatize the text, radical variations of type size and treatment within a limited typeface vocabulary are used. Anchoring the compositions are a standard smaller text size and repeated abstract elements that define the interior 6" square format.

1

The subject must not realize that the mistreatment is a deliberate attack of an anti-human enemy on his personal identity.

He must be made to feel that he deserves any treatment he receives because there is something horribly wrong with him.

C.5 combined with another icon ▲

2

Junk yields a basic formula of "evil" virus:

The
Algebra
of
Need.

$\times$ πr^2 ? $+$ $=$

The face of "evil" is always the face of total need. A dope fiend is a man in total need of dope. Beyond a certain frequency, need knows absolutely no limit or control.

C.5 combined with another icon ▲

C.5, C.6 combined with another icon and texture ▼

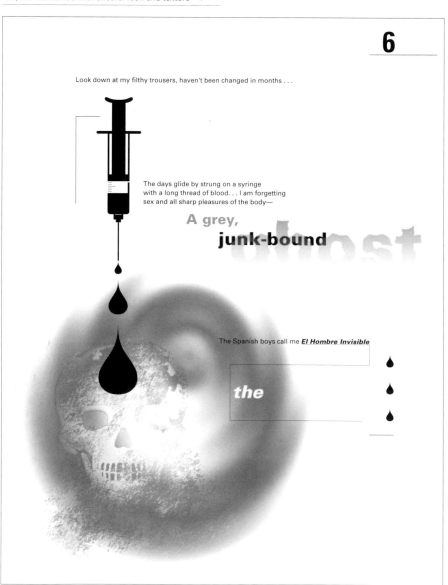

6

Look down at my filthy trousers, haven't been changed in months . . .

The days glide by strung on a syringe with a long thread of blood. . . I am forgetting sex and all sharp pleasures of the body—

A grey,
junk-bound ghost

The Spanish boys call me *El Hombre Invisible*

the

The body knows

what veins you can hit and conveys
this knowledge in the spontaneous movements you
make preparing to take a shot. . . . Sometimes the
needle points like a dowser's wand. Sometimes I must
wait for the message. But when it comes, I always
hit blood.

A.2, C.1 deconstruction as chance, combined with ▲
actual object

forms:

Addiction

The needle is not important.

Whether you sniff it smoke it eat it
it or shove it up your ass the result is
the same.

A.6.a repetition/ornamental ▲

Shoot it in the mainline, son.

You can smell it going in, clean
and cold in your nose and throat then a rush
of pure pleasure right through the brain
lighting up those C connections. Your head
shatters in white explosions.

Ten minutes later you want another shot.

C.3 combined with hand/functional ▲

E.3 other: combined with face/functional, deconstruc-
tion/functional, combined with other symbol ▼

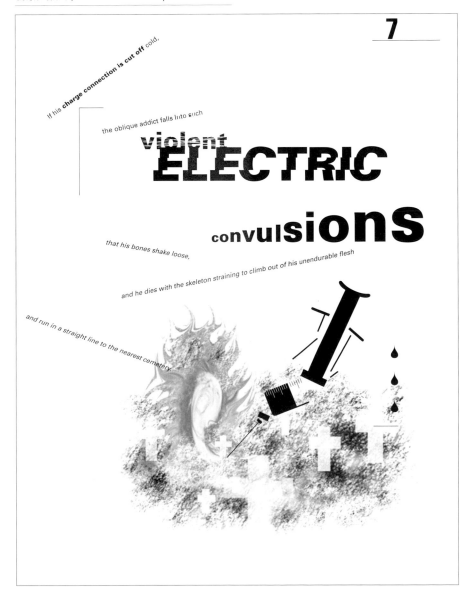

If his charge connection is cut off cold,

the oblique addict falls into such

violent ELECTRIC

convulsions

that his bones shake loose,

and he dies with the skeleton straining to climb out of his unendurable flesh

and run in a straight line to the nearest cemetery.

8

More and more static at the Drug
Store, mutterings of control like a telephone
off the hook. . . . Spent all day until 8 p.m. to
score for two more boxes of Eukodol. . . .

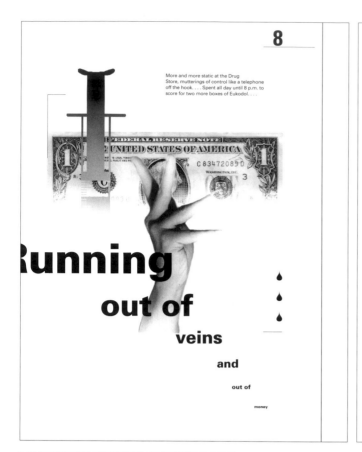

Running

out of

veins

and

out of

money

E.3 other: combined with hand/formal and other   ▲
contrasting image

9

Well the buyer comes to look more and
more like a junky.

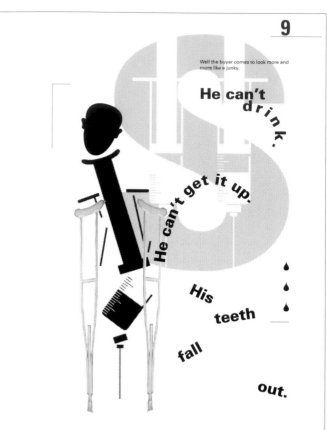

He can't
d r i n k.

He can't get it up.

His

teeth

fall

out.

D.1 as metaphor for human body   ▲

C.8 placed in another time or culture   ▼

Buddha? A notorious
metabolic junky . . . Makes his
own you dig. In India, where
they got no sense of time, The
Man is often a month late. . . .
'Now let me see, is that the
second or the third monsoon?
I got like a meet in
Ketchupore about more or
less.'

And all them junkies
sitting around in the lotus
posture spitting on the ground
and awaiting on The Man.

"So Buddha says: 'I don't
hafta take this sound.
I'll by God metabolize my
own junk.'

Addicts can be cured or quarantined—
that is, allowed a morphine ration under minimal
supervision, like typhoid carriers.

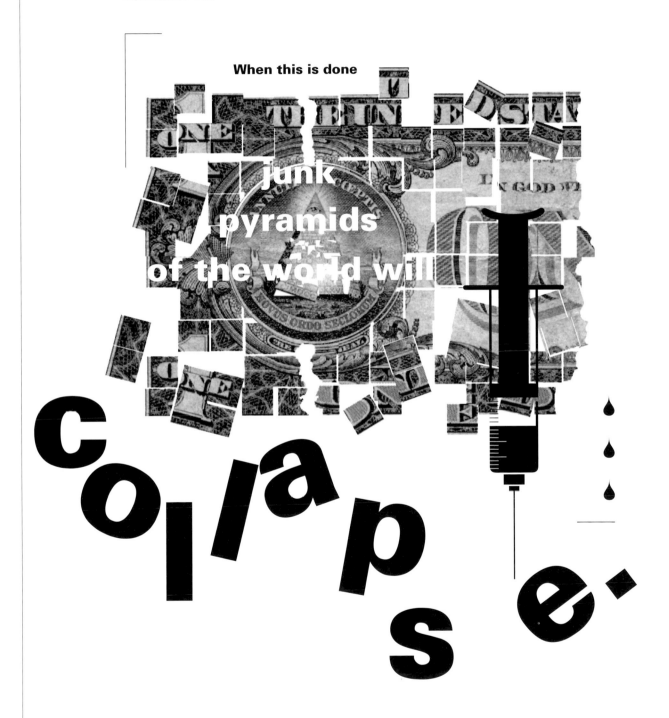

When this is done

junk
pyramids
of the world will

collapse

E.3 other: combined with action word, related
form/contrasting funtion (pyramid and syringe with
points), deconstruction as function

Icon base: clown

Series concept:
Texts are descriptions of Charlie Chaplin movies developed by a student from personal research and viewing of the films.

Typographic concept:
A single type column maintains constant left margin except for one line, which is isolated for emphasis and positioned to relate to the overall composition.

3

Raved by many critics as being Chaplin's first successful attempt at motion pictures, *The Tramp* quickly became known amongst worldwide audiences. One British journal of the time, *Bioscope*, said of Chaplin during the release of this film, "an exceptionally hard worker, his natural genius is always seen to the best advantage . . .and his

carefully calculated effects

never fail to come off."

Circa 1915, Silent feature.

The

Tramp

C.6 combined with related texture ▲

5

This one-reel film does more for Chaplin's on-screen machismo than any other past or future releases. Charlie, in an unusual role, incorporates characteristics of **the confidence trickster and sycophantic lover** and eventually wins . . . on both sides? In fact, as he makes off with his prize-catch-of-the-day, a naive nursemaid he encounters in the park (and her lover's pocketbook), all his adversaries are left wading in the pond as Charlie obligingly throws a few blows at each man. It is of course springtime, and every dog has his day. But Charlie undoubtedly went down in history for being one of the most virile men with an insatiable appetite for love and romance.

Released 1915, silent feature.

A.4 distortion of a part ▲   A.6.c repetition/random ▼

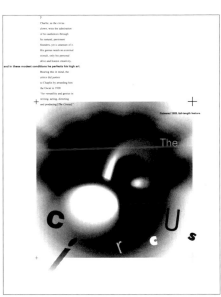

7

Charlie, as the circus clown, wins the admiration of his audiences through his natural, persistent blunders, yet is unaware of it. His genius needs no external stimuli, only his personal drive and honest creativity, **and in these modest conditions he perfects his high art.** Bearing this in mind, the critics did justice to Chaplin by awarding him the Oscar in 1928 "for versatility and genius in writing, acting, directing and producing [The Circus]."

Released 1928, full-length feature.

E.3 other: blur + noun ▲

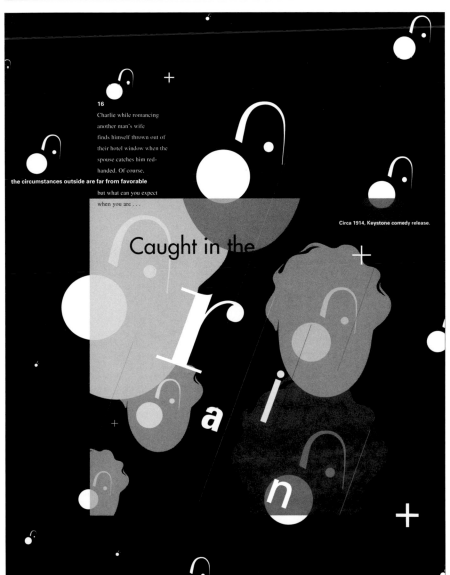

16

Charlie while romancing another man's wife finds himself thrown out of their hotel window when the spouse catches him red-handed. Of course, **the circumstances outside are far from favorable** but what can you expect when you are . . .

Caught in the

r
a
i
n

Circa 1914, Keystone comedy release.

4

Though Chaplin was
consistent with his tramp
image on screen,
occasionally he resorted to
more ludicrous trans-
formations for furthering his
clownish impact on
his conservative audiences.
His art was not always well-
received and W.C. Fields
once said of him,
"he's a g__d__ ballet dancer."
On the other hand Shaw
extolled his work, citing that
"he is the one genius created
by the cinema."

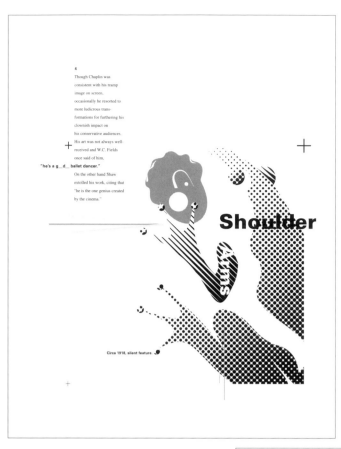

Shoulder Arms

Circa 1918, silent feature.

C.1 combined with actual image photo ▼

C.5 combined with another icon (frog) ▲

8

Calvero (Charlie Chaplin)
is a traditional clown
who is being made redundant
because of his old age.
His key note resounds with
one theme:
"the bittersweet contact between the audience and the drama."
Although many critics have
found flaw with *Limelight*, a
great many believe
that the film, congruous
to Chaplin's face, projects
"an emotional spectrum
of variations."

Limelight

1952, full-length sound feature.

12

Once Chaplin boasted to the press that "all [he] needed to make a picture was a park, a policeman, and a pretty girl." This statement was refuted by his masterpiece over two decades later when *Modern Times* dictated that

life no longer was a paradise

but, rather, involved the chaos and the aftermath of a highly industrialized era that crushed individuality and left very little room for human contact.

Modern

Times

1936, silent feature, musical score.

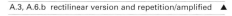

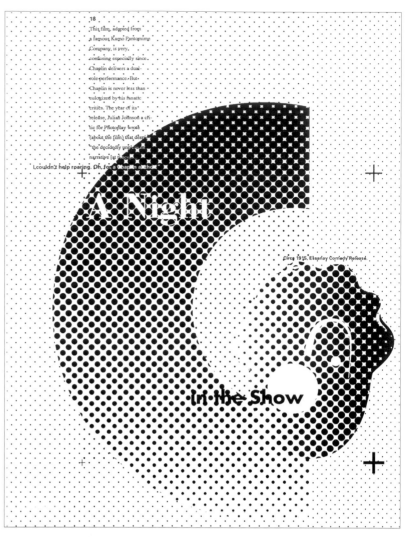

18

This film, adapted from a famous Karno Pantomime Company, is very confusing especially since Chaplin delivers a dual-role performance. But Chaplin is never less than eulogized by his fanatic critics. The year of its release, Julian Johnson a critic for Photoplay wrote (about the film) that described "the decidedly universal narrative [at times] I couldn't help roaring. Oh, for a Chaplin a-day."

A Night

Circa 1915, Essanlay Comedy Release.

In the Show

C.2 combined with letter form ▲

C.8 placed in another culture and time ▼

A.6.a repetition/ornamental ▼

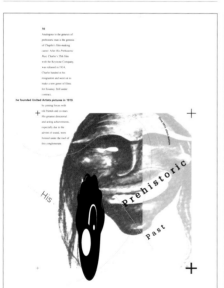

16

Analogous to the genesis of prehistoric man is the genesis of Chaplin's film-making career. After His Prehistoric Past, Charlie's 35th film with the Keystone Company, was released in 1914, Charlie handed in his resignation and went on to make a new genre of films for Essanay. Still under contract,

he founded United Artists pictures in 1919 by joining forces with old friends and co-stars. His greatest directorial and acting achievements, especially due to the advent of sound, were formed under the roof of this conglomerate.

His

Prehistoric

Past

17

As *The Immigrant*, Charlie is onboard a ship to America, loaded with other people also in search of a dream. In New York, he has his first and worst experience in a restaurant, where he realizes at the end of his meal that he cannot settle his damages. His narrow escape from the menacing waiter is hilarious, in fact as one of Chaplin's biographers writes it is "one of **the longest scenes of brilliantly suspended comedy** in all of Chaplin's films."

14

Our ubiquitous Charlie is pondering the idea of suicide. The decision is the result of his lacking female companionship, but the scenario changes rapidly as a beautiful girl crosses his path. In her wake she brings a jealous boyfriend, two insane policemen, and a brick-throwing battle. Amidst the "recreation" and turmoil,

"Charlie has opportunities to renew his ardent flirtation"

and becomes victorious as he pushes his adversaries into the lake.

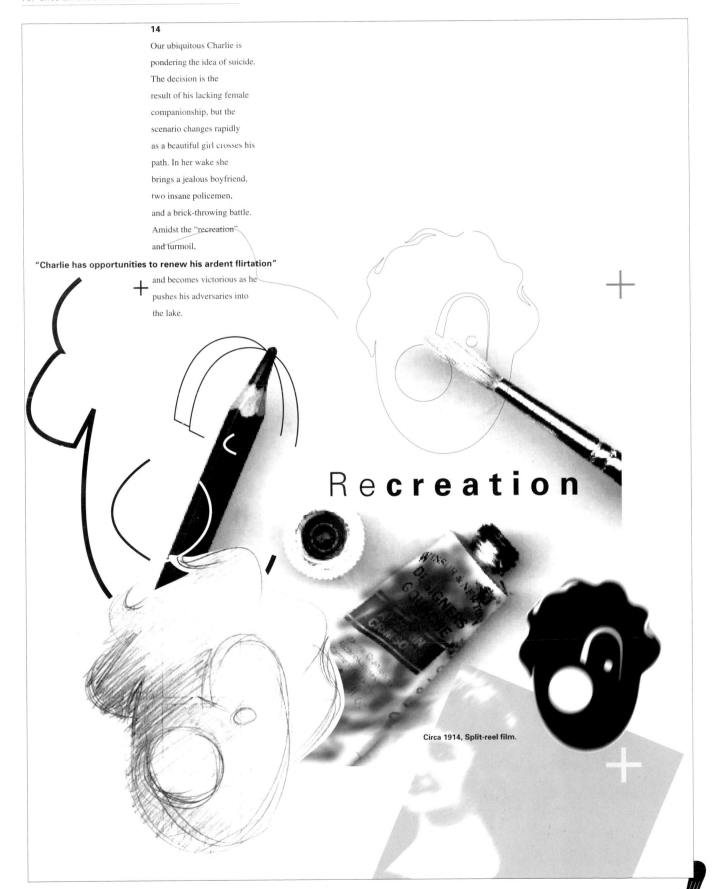

R e **c r e a t i o n**

Circa 1914, Split-reel film.

19

The emotional quagmire of
married life portrayed in
this film is astoundingly real,
yet the sequence of events
presented creates a form
of enjoyment undeniable in
all of Chaplin's films. A critic
suggests that enjoying this
film might take a certain
amount of
scrutiny of "the incongruity of Chaplin's portrayals . . ."
Besides being a hen-
pecked husband, Charlie
cannot cope with
fatherhood and is suspect in a
love tryst by his domi-
neering wife, but eventually
all misunderstandings
are resolved.

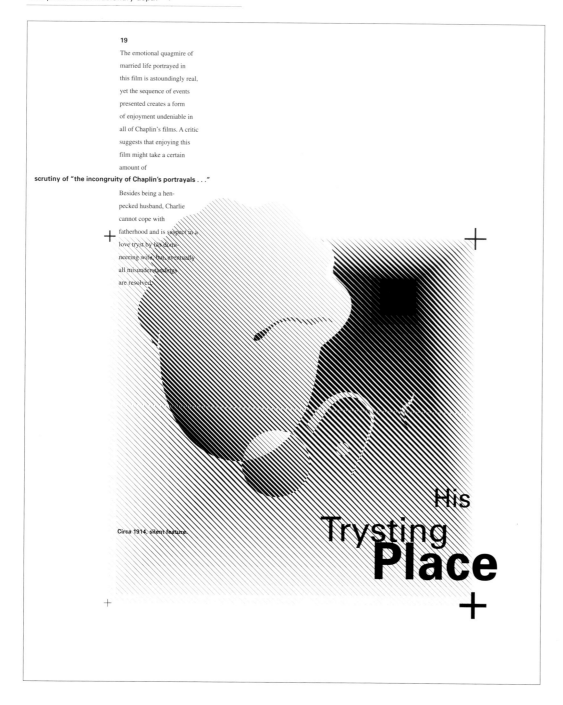

Circa 1914, silent feature.

His
Trysting
Place

Drawing from . . .

Music

People are born with the ability to create and respond to rhythm. Music epitomizes rhythmic form. In music, we easily grasp rhythm's abstract quality, which is based on fundamental relations among defined units. Rhythm and other features of music give the visual designer a vocabulary, criteria, and inspiration for forms that elicit strong emotional responses.

▼

This chapter explores ways we use music as source, stimulus, and influence for graphic image making. The range of experiences documented includes:

building a visual vocabulary as an analogue to musical ideas and terms and using this experience to create a graphic identity and promotional applications for a musical ensemble;

·

interpreting four types of music by making images in direct response to listening to the music; and

·

using a listening experience to set the stage for a communication in which contexts are merged.

The extreme opposite of matter is music—not possible without utterances of physical beings or vibrations of physical things, still not in the least descriptive of their physicality, a delight only to the spirit, victorious over dumb matter, lifting high above, freed, spatial and matter-less, a pure joy beyond pain and disintegration, surviving all in memory.

The Irreconcilable Second and Fourth Dimensions:
The differences between music and visual design are fundamental. The average person cannot "take in" a musical piece of any typical duration the way he or she can take in a two-dimensional painting or graphic work. The traversing of a piece of music is like walking in the woods at a tempo beyond our control, noticing in turn this flower or that bird or those rocks or that reflection, the relation of rocks to reflections to trees, each experience superseding the previous one. In contrast, traversing a two-dimensional image is more like looking down on the terrain covered by the walk, seeing the whole pattern, entering the land anywhere one can or wishes, seeing each detail in the simultaneous context of the whole, now the rocks, now the stream, now the birds, and each in relation to the other, lingering wherever one wishes for as long as one wants.

The music composer hopes that the procession of experiences will cumulatively build a gestalt of a certain distinct character; the visual artist hopes that this gestalt character will present itself forcefully enough to invite the viewer into the procession of events contained within the larger image. The composer is assured of the sequence of events (disturbed only by the wandering attention of the listener), whereas the visual artist has less assurance that a viewer (who decides what to look at when) will spend any time with a piece beyond an initial glance.

The visual artist could envy the composer of music for several reasons:

Music is made of rhythm, and rhythm seems to be the universal human language. Movement equates to life, and movement of a definite rhythm brings life to a state of eloquence and elegance. Rhythm is what we are seeking within each image

> *"All art aspires to the condition of music."*
> —Johann Wolfgang von Goethe

and sequence of images. Rhythm is equally a function of form and space with the space between beats as determining as the beat itself. The lesson for visual form-making is that by rhythmically changing any recurrence of form the eye never fixates on any part. Instead, the eye is prompted to see all the rest because change invites peregrinations.

Music is unbounded by spatial constraints and readily transcends the physical, the goal of most art. Music can sustain in the face of severe physical deprivation. Song has the power to lift spirits. Music functions in the realm of the spirit.

Music has freer reign to use abstraction than visual art, where the validity of abstraction is not taken for granted. This holds true whether music is classical or popular. In music we don't question a purely instrumental piece. Symphonies, concertos, and sonatas—as well as jigs, reels, and polkas—have long inspired audiences of great diversity and number. A Bach partita for violin, a Shostakovich prelude and fugue, and Joseph Schwantner's *Distant Runes and Incantations* each exists as a compelling abstraction. Their audiences may not be large compared to those of easier to grasp pop music, but they are international and durable.

Music's notational system allows music of the greatest emotional depth to be expressed with an objective, systematic, shared structure. Visual literacy is less codified and a constant subject of debate. The ability to describe a piece in structural terms balances the tendency to compare it in stylistic terms. In visual design, it is easy and tempting to identify something as, say, in the style of Cassandre or El Lissitzky, as Swiss or Cranbrook, rather than describing the structural means at work. Although attempts to codify visual language in a way akin to that of music have never yielded anything but skepticism about the possibility for a unified approach to visual literacy, the search for objective expression—communication, in other words— is ongoing and a primary concern of education.

Music as a Stimulus to Visual Form-Making

Music can influence visual form in various ways:

1. *Musical notation and methods of composition can show the visual artist ways of thinking about formal relationships in another way, as encoded in notation conventions.* Applying the language of one discipline to another has a distinct danger—that of the amateur out of his or her element— but it also has the advantage of newness, of a spark of recognition, of another way to think about something. Music itself has benefited, as Susanne K. Langer points out in *Mind: An Essay on Human Feelings*, from borrowed terms, from metaphors and descriptors of linguistic origin. The experiment of finding visual equivalents for basic musical terms allows students to see design from another perspective and to become sensitive to parallels (and their perils!) and serves as a warm-up for interpretive work. It awakens, loosens, exercises.

For example, converting a mixed row of letters and dots to rhythmic configurations of distinct kinds, bringing them into a counterpoint, produces a fresh structure of form and a "musical" feel:

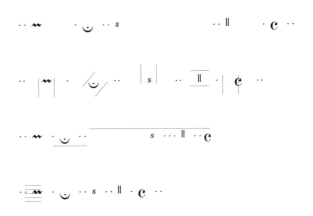

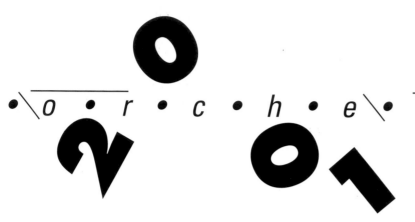

The range of musical terms and qualities chosen for the exercises beginning on page 97 is a limited selection from the vast vocabulary and nuance in music theory and practice. The terms chosen seem appropriate to me for students with little or no prior acquaintance with music from this perspective. Yet these terms are just words, not music, and they need to be heard as musical expression. I like to use Carl Orff's *Music for Children* as a way to introduce designers progressively to the fundamentals of musical form. Each step is demonstrated in sound, *performed with a spirit that transcends the exercise.*

2. *Listening to music can establish a transcendent emotional plane that substantially affects visual quality.* So argues anyone who thinks he or she works better tuned in to music. But we need to distinguish between osmotic absorption of music—music as mere ambiance or soporific indulgence—and listening as experience. A teacher once told me that the modern music the conductor Paul Sacher was constantly introducing to the Basel public was troublesome until he decided to really *listen*; suddenly the music became an *Ohrenschmaus,* a treat for the ears. Anyone who listens with prejudices of one's peer values, pop culture fads, or long familiarity will find it hard to hear the truly new in pure music. In my use of music, I look for a range of sources, but ones that I think will be unfamiliar to my students. The more familiar the piece is, the less it stimulates. Students who develop a dependence on music while working often think that they are working better, but their work is actually often weaker than when they are fully concentrated and energized. Listening to unfamiliar music demands real hearing in order to make sense out of it; it provokes a different kind of listening from the usual headphone addiction. The students may not like what they hear, but they will listen.

3. *Listening can be the source of a visual interpretation of the music.* The designer who creates the visual tools for marketing recorded or live music works in a fashion that is only slightly different from designing a dust jacket for a book: content is encapsulated. Often, of course, such designs are related to the content only tangentially; they are frequently the product of marketing ploys to place the product in a certain category rather than authentically revealing.

An authentic experience is the goal, but it is hard to authenticate! In looking at interpretations of the same music produced by different people, we see that each has captured some aspect, has heard it in some way, that each is authentic because it is made without reference to other outside influences during the design process. This confirms that in the realm of both music and the visual arts—as compared to the verbal realm—qualities abound and a common interpretation would be unthinkable.

"The limitations inherent in verbal conception and discursive forms of thought are the very raison d'être of artistic expression; to surpass those limitations requires the abandonment of the activity which entails them, and which tends to interfere with the more precarious process of implementing formal intuitions of another kind than those usually called 'logical': the process of perceiving and rendering the forms of feeling which are not amenable to generalizing abstraction."—Susanne K. Langer

In these ways music has been used to stimulate form-making in this chapter.

Music's Link to Abstraction

Vision is connected to the world so literally that literal visualization is more familiar and trusted by the average person than sound. Sound is a more sporadic and chaotic element of our environment, and the musician's function in bringing abstract order to sound is generally sensed. The kinetic action of music as it unfolds conveys the feeling that something is happening whether one "understands" that activity or not.

to reproduce
the work in another
medium . . . this
hope has never been
realized. Kandinsky's
principles of
projection illustrate
one of the major
difficulties of such
undertakings:
the interpreter con-
ceives works
technically in only
one of the two
arts he compares.
In this case he sees
(visual) works
with a professional
eye, but what
he hears in music is
what an amateur
hears: rhythmic
figuration, timbre,
general levels of
pitch and dynamics.
. . . Despite all
these difficulties,
however, it is
hard to shake off
the conviction that

'sensuous' metaphor
does play some
important role in
art. ...only we have
to determine what
different sensations
really do have an
emotive character
in common."
—Susanne K. Langer

"After silence
that which comes
nearest to
expressing the
inexpressible is
music."
—Aldous Huxley

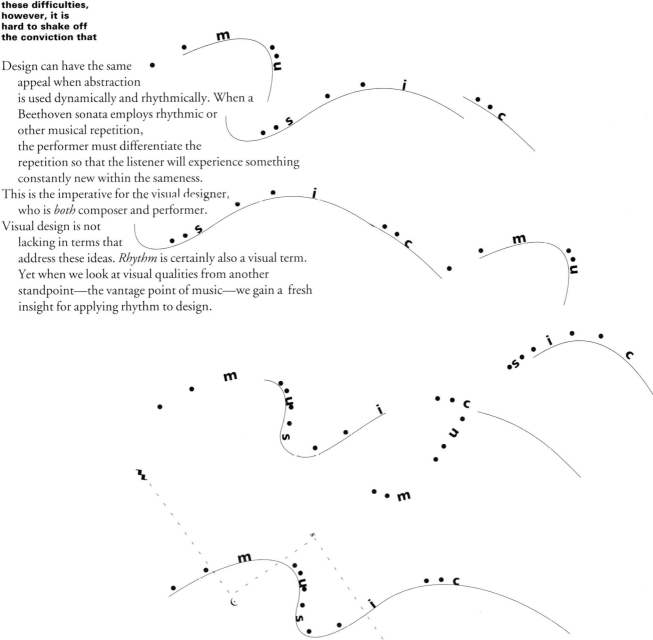

Design can have the same
    appeal when abstraction
    is used dynamically and rhythmically. When a
    Beethoven sonata employs rhythmic or
    other musical repetition,
    the performer must differentiate the
    repetition so that the listener will experience something
    constantly new within the sameness.
This is the imperative for the visual designer,
    who is *both* composer and performer.
Visual design is not
    lacking in terms that
    address these ideas. *Rhythm* is certainly also a visual term.
    Yet when we look at visual qualities from another
    standpoint—the vantage point of music—we gain a fresh
    insight for applying rhythm to design.

Music Project 1:
Orchestra 2001,
Studies and Application
Background:

Orchestra 2001 is a musical ensemble that performs new music written for classically based musicians and instruments as well as innovative and experimental scores that do not fit the narrow definition of classical music.

The music director tells the students about the orchestra's special identity as an exponent of new or seldom heard music in the classical realm. The small ensemble performs composed new music, not improvisational music. Its eclectic repertory includes pieces that incorporate vocal soloists as well as purely instrumental works.

The pieces Orchestra 2001 performs are generally difficult technically and require a great deal of memorization. Each score has a different character, often strongly visual, which aids the performers' memory. The ensemble's programs aim to combine culture and entertainment while making this "difficult" music accessible.

The musical director next describes the pieces the students will hear. (None of the students has a background or developed interest in classical music.)

Diadem, composed by Louise Talma in 1980 at age seventy-five, is, according to the director, a "spare, serious, elegant, not tuneful, beautifully constructed" interpretation of the symbolic meaning of gems—jade, aquamarine, ruby, topaz, diamond, sapphire, and emerald.

Distant Runes and Incantations, composed by Joseph Schwantner in 1986, is a "neo-romantic piece filled with beautiful sounds. A water gong, immersed in water while sounding, provides the sound aura for the piece. It is generally easy to grasp."

Aubade, created in 1992 by Thomas Whitman, was commissioned by the orchestra's artistic director for his wife, an oboist with Orchestra 2001. It combines English horn with "lots of bell sounds—glockenspiel, gongs, tam-tams, vibraphone—plus tympani and rattles."

The Daniel Jazz, op. 21, by Louis Gruenberg, who "thought composed music should reflect popular music," was composed in 1924. A tenor soloist sings a poem by Vachel Lindsay that dramatizes the Old Testament story of Daniel in informal, vernacular terms.

With this brief and animated presentation by the orchestra's director, the class is primed to attend the concert.

Process:
1.
We enter the world of music by studying a selection of musical terms and concepts. The words stem from standard classical music vocabulary and twentieth-century innovation.
Terms selected for these exercises:
accent
amplitude
chord
counterpoint
cues
duration
improvisation
interval
legato
major/minor key
mathematical pattern
melodic theme
operations:
    inversion
    retrograde-inversion
    retrograde
ostinato
pitch change
polyrhythm
rhythm
staccato
syncopation
timbre
tone clusters

After defining these terms verbally we move to visual equivalents, beginning on the facing page.
The preliminary exercises were in part predefined by choices of typefaces made by the students.
These were:

Typeface	Example
Garamond 3 Roman	music
New Baskerville Roman	music
Bauer Bodoni Italic	*music*
Poster Bodoni	**music**
New Century Schoolbook	music
Glypha Bold	**music**
Futura Light	music
Univers Condensed Oblique	*music*
Frutiger Black	**music**
Helvetica Compressed Extra	music
Futura Extra Bold	**music**
Sonata	♪ ♩ s ‖ C

Each typeface colors the resulting structure differently. This, plus the students' handling of the themes, gradually produces individuality of response.
The Sonata typeface for musical notation feels inherently musical; yet "musicality" is expressed by spatial relations at least as much as in the "instrumentation," as the examples show.
2.
The class meets with the musical director as described under Background.
3.
Students develop a logotype for the orchestra using the studies in step 1 as preparation.
4.
The class attends the concert described under Background. One work, **Distant Runes and Incantations,** *by Joseph Schwantner, is chosen as the basis of a visual interpretation.*
5.
Students work on a series of applications from stationery to programs to banners. A CD package containing four of the works is designed in all its aspects. The words **distant runes** *are extrapolated for the title from Schwantner's composition.*

1.
Rhythmic patterns

The studies use 15
elements, 10 dots plus
m u s i c .
Version 1 is based on
Univers Condensed
Oblique.

1.1
A regular **rhythm** of 15
elements.

• • m • u • s • i • c • • • •

1.2
Varied **duration** from
short to sustained.

•• m • u • s i c • • • •

1.3
Changes of **interval**
applied to 1.1.

• •m •u• s •i •c• • ••

1.4
The pattern **syncopated**,
accented on unexpected
beats.

• •m •u• s •i • c• • ••

1.5
A **variation** on the
rhythmic theme.

• • m•u•s•i•c • • • •

1.6
A rhythmic **improvisa-
tion** that transcends the
rhythmic pattern.

• •m • u • s •i • c• • ••

1.7
A **polyrhythm** formed by
relating two rhythmic
patterns in a single
structure.

• •m • u • s •i • c• • ••
• •m •u• s •i •c• • ••

1.8
Cues or **accents** inserted.

> • • m • u • s •i• > c• • • • •

2.
**Melodic theme with
pitch changes
and operations on the
theme**

2.1
Elements placed on a
curved line to form a
prime **melodic theme** using a
rhythmic idea.

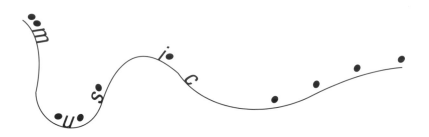

2.2
Operations of **inversion,
retrograde,** and
retrograde-inversion
performed on the prime
theme. (As in music,
these are intelligible only
when introduced by the
prime melodic theme.)

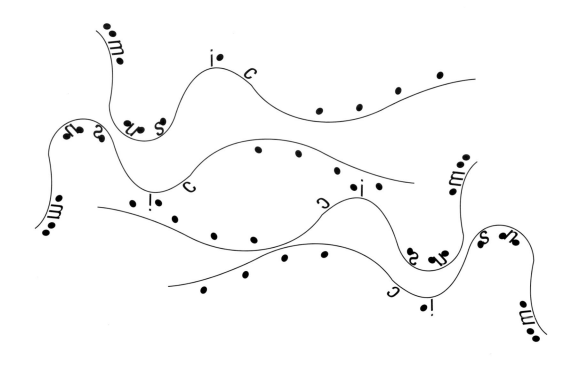

2.3
The prime melodic theme
broken further into
phrases.

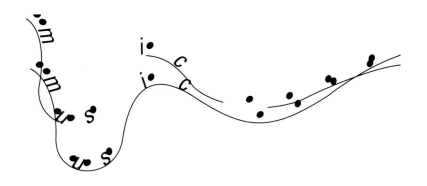

2.4
Phrased another way.

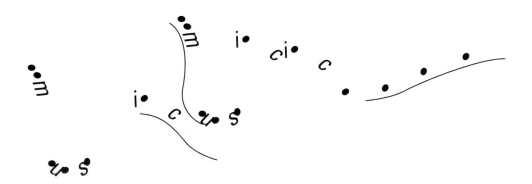

2.5
A **counterpoint** rhythm in relation to the prime theme.

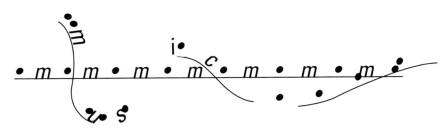

2.6
A **staccato-legato** contrast in the melody.

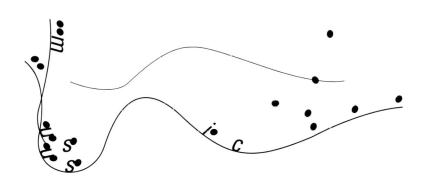

2.7
The **amplitude** of the elements increased:

a. gradually

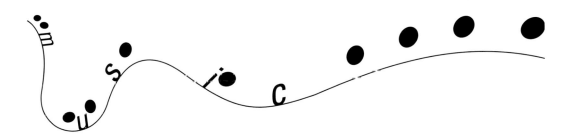

b. suddenly.

2.8
The **timbre** (color) within the note structure changed.

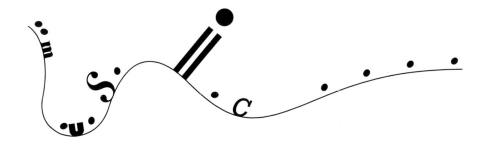

3.
Tone clusters and operations on a cluster

3.1
Tones of varying timbre and amplitude around a home tone (**tonal center**), arranged sequentially. Linearity sacrificed.

3.2
Arranged as a chord (single composite element).

3.3
The arrangement shifted to a **minor key**—like adding the excitement of sourness to something sweet.

3.4
A **cluster-dispersal** contrast applied to the composite element.

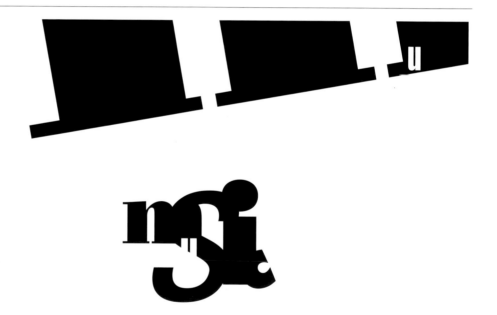

4.
Combinations

4.1
Ostinato (repetitious)
rhythm combined with an
expressive theme.

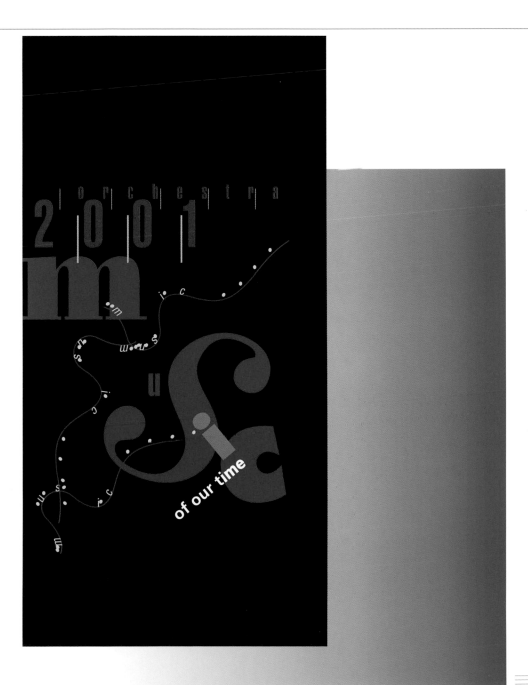

4.2
Exotic color within an
expressive theme,
combined with logo
design in a banner
application.

Selections from studies
based on changes
in typeface (timbre).

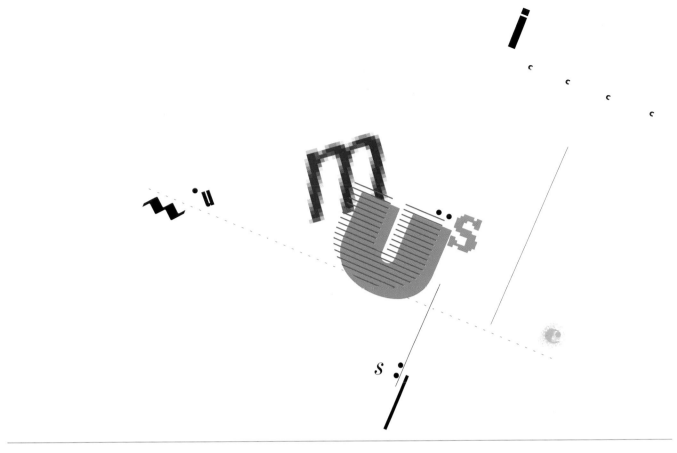

Louise Talma, Diadem (1980)
Joseph Schwantner, Distant Runes and Incantations (1986)
Thomas Whitman, Aubade (1992)
Louis Gruenberg, The Daniel Jazz (1924)

James Freeman, conductor
Paul Sperry, tenor
Charles Abramovic, piano
Dorothy Freeman, English horn

Digital Stereo

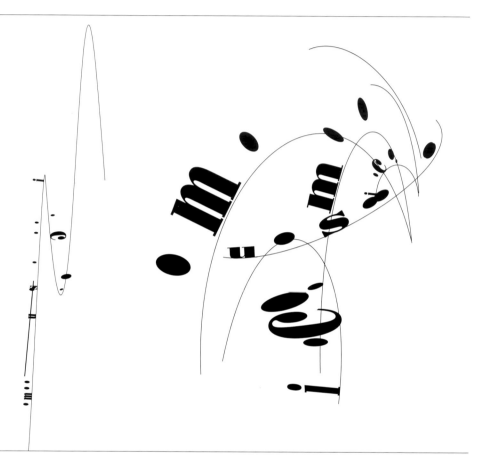

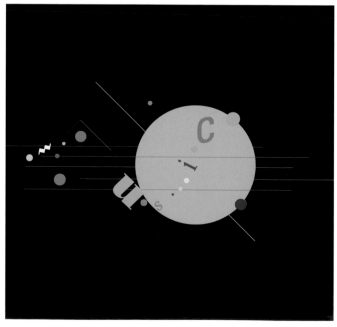

Louise Talma
Diadem (1980) 14:28
1 Jade 3:13
2 Aquamarine 1:15
3 Ruby 4:02
4 Topaz 2:03
5 Diamond 1:54
6 Sapphire :30
7 Emerald 1:46

Joseph Schwantner
8 Distant Runes and
Incantations (1986) 15:15

orchestra 2001

distant

≡CRI
digital stereo

RUNES

Thomas Whitman
9 Aubade (1992) 18:10

Louis Gruenberg
10 The Daniel Jazz,
Op. 21 (1924) 15:12

.orchestra 2001

distant

RUNES

Selections from studies
based on Helvetica Extra
Compressed.

M • • • u • s • • • i • • c • •

M • • • u • s • • • i • • c •

M • • • — u • s • • • — i • • c •

M • • • u • — s • • • i • • c •

M • | • • • u • s ||| • • • i • • | c | || •

M | • • — • ||| • — s • • — • i • | • c | • —

M • • • • u • s • • • i • • c • •

M̄ • • • u • — s • • • i • • c ⁄ •

Orchestra 2001

Orchestra 2001

Distant Runes

2 0 0 1

CRI Digital Stereo

Music Project 2:
7x7 Workshop, listening while drawing on a computer

Background:
Students were given a computer file containing a predrawn seven-inch square field and instructions at the head of the field. We played and replayed a series of three short pieces during the process of interpretation. The goal was to work spontaneously and quickly, allowing fifteen to thirty minutes for each study.

Theme 1, Source and Process:

Carl Orff, Music for Children

The music is a percussion piece with increasingly complex rhythms. A grid of dots segmented into three columns is furnished.

The instructions:
To reflect the music you hear, add rules and other dot elements. Delete some of the grid dots, if desired. Integrate the title "Orff Music for Children" in any typeface or size.

Use the grid to make the rhythmic shifts transparently clear.

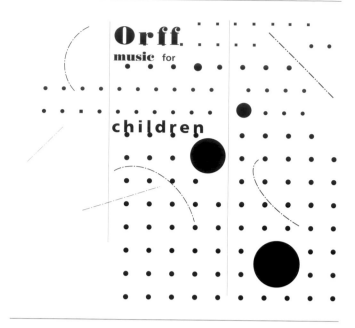

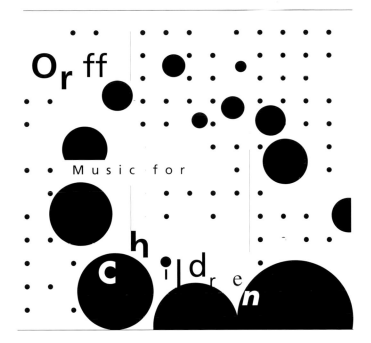

Orff

Music for

Children

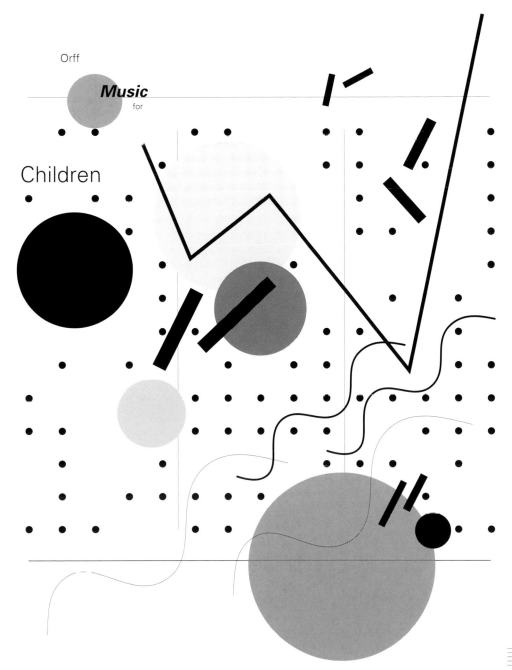

Theme 2, Source and Process:

Bach, Prelude and Fugue, no. 13

This prelude is gentle and seemingly simple, increasing in complexity but never losing a compelling lilt. The piano unifies the musical lines.

The instructions state:
Decide the typeface, size, and position of the name "Bach" and add rule lines of your choosing to reflect a quality you perceive in this Prelude and Fugue.

(Within any piece of music it is possible to identify and focus on very different aspects, from the smooth and graceful to the angularity of counterpoint. Thus, although none of the interpretations is true to the whole piece, each is true in some important respect.)

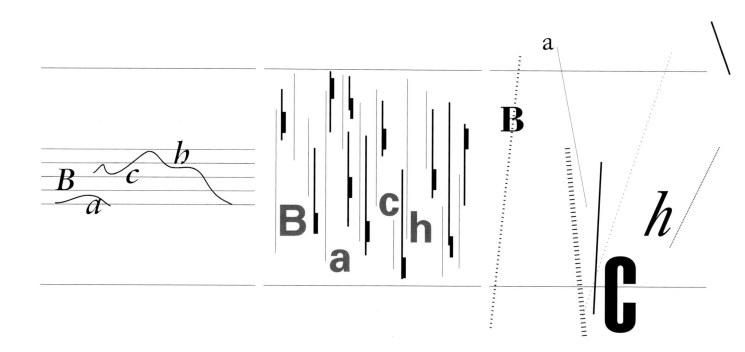

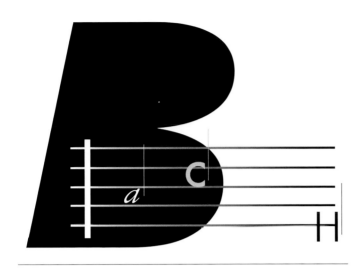

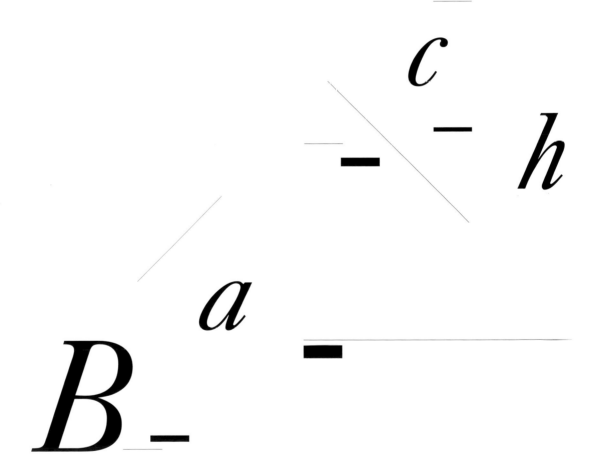

Theme 3, Source and Process:

*Gender Wayang, Ansarun
(from "Music from the Morning of the
World")*

*Xylophone- and marimba-like instru-
ments create an accompaniment for
shadow plays. The instruments' ringing
sounds resonate through bamboo
tubes. This music is based on a five-tone
scale.*

*The instructions:
Position and scale the four following
elements in response to the sounds of
this music:*

*Add a contrasting and repeated element
and create a composition that reflects
the Balinese Gender Wayang. Incorporate
the word "Bali" in an appropriate type
style.*

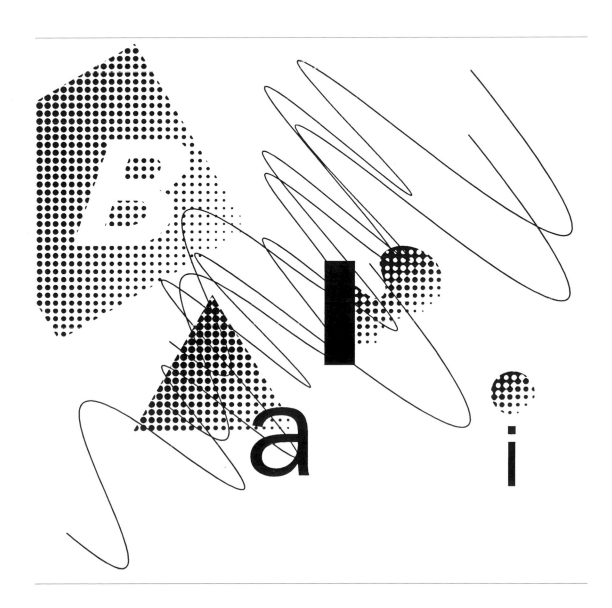

Music Project 3:

Black Angels
five pieces performed by the Kronos
Quartet

Background:
The tone of the music is somber and
sometimes piercing, as in the opening
composition by George Crumb,
which forms the title of the album.
In an allusion to the Vietnam War, the
music unleashes "electric insects."

Process:
We listened to the music in a dark room
lit by a single candle. Students
noted in words or images the feelings
they experienced. Letter forms were used
to capture the overall sense of the
performance. The character of the central
motif was applied in designing other
components of a CD package.

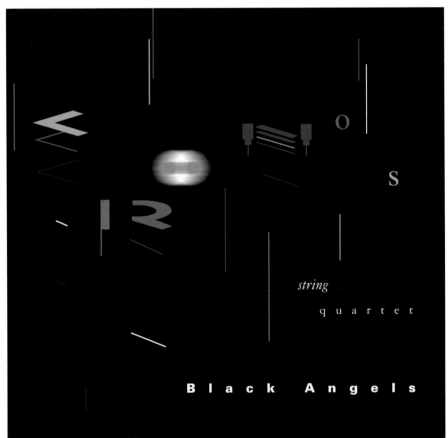

Music Project 4:
Convergence of multiple influences
beginning with music as a stimulus
(A continuation of the transformational
programs project in chapter 2)

Process:
1.
While listening to music, certain ab-
stract elements were combined with a
previously designed icon to create
a composition that reflects the students'
response.
The composition was completed as a
black-and-white assemblage within a set
time of approximately thirty minutes. See
the process summary at the foot of each
page beginning at page 118.
(Note that the same elements may be
used as a base for different music.)
2.
In a conversion to color, done as a follow-
up, and in the addition of text, designs
developed a specific meaning. The
persistence of the music as the original
stimulus varies in strength depending on
the new meaning that was found.

Themes for these compositions are:

Theme 1.
"O quam mirabilis est," by Hildegard
von Bingen (1098–1179)
"How wondrous is the prescience of
the divine Heart . . . ," a vocal expression
of supreme loftiness and serenity.

Theme 2.
Adagio cantabile, third movement from
Sonata no. 3, op. 69, for cello and
piano, by Ludwig van Beethoven, 1807,
with a lush romantic beginning that leads
to an exuberant outburst.

Theme 3.
"The Dancing Sorcerer," from *Planet
Drum,* by Mickey Hart, 1991.

Theme 4.
Echoes, by John Lunn, 1980, an integration of piano and computer-generated
sound as an aural extension of the piano's
capabilities.

Theme 5.
Tabula Rasa, by Arvo Pärt, 1989.
Themes 5 and 6 are preceded by a reading
of Pärt's description of his going back to a
basic source, the triad:

> "In my dark hours, I have the certain
> feeling that everything outside this one
> thing has no meaning. The complex
> and many-faceted only confuses me,
> and I must search for unity. What is it,
> this one thing, and how do I find my
> way to it? Traces of this perfect thing
> appear in many guises—and everything
> that is unimportant falls away.
> . . . Here I am alone with silence. I have
> discovered that it is enough when a
> single note is beautifully played. This
> one note, or a silent beat, or a moment
> of silence, comforts me. I work with
> very few elements—with one voice,
> two voices. I build with the most
> primitive materials—with the triad with
> one specific tonality . . . the three
> notes of a triad."

Theme 6.
"Miserere," by Arvo Pärt, 1989, a liturgical
work opening with words from Psalm 51,
a psalm of repentance.

Theme 7.
"They," from *The Search for It and Other
Pronouns,* by Harvey Goldman and Warren Lehrer, 1991. "They" is a riotous pop
cantata segment with the theme of para-
noia—"They did it to me! . . . and they
could do it to you." They—those others
who lurk, who threaten, who distract and
confuse, surprise and overwhelm—are
not hard to find in relation to any of the
students' themes.

Example for theme 7, facing page:
The given elements and icon are composed
while the student listens to the music. The
image is translated into color. A text in accord
with the theme of the icon transformation
project see (chapter 2) is found and applied.
Function largely follows form because meaning
is sought in the image that results from the
music-listening experience.

Given elements:
—The word *they* in a range of fourteen type
styles
—!? punctuation marks

Elements furnished by student:
—fingerprint icon
—a text found to be appropriate in accord
with an overall theme of Sigmund Freud and
personal identity

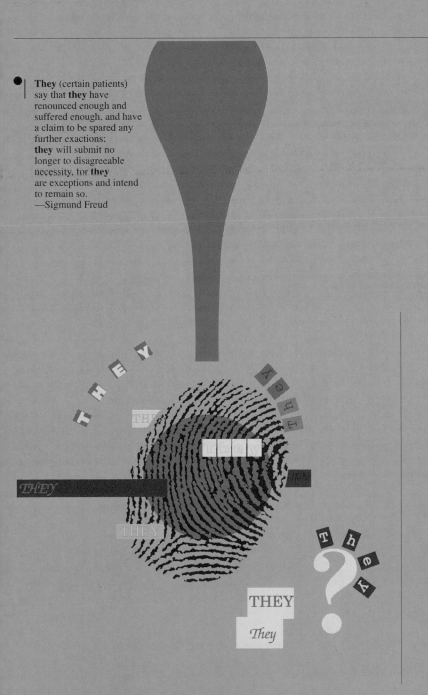

> **They** (certain patients) say that **they** have renounced enough and suffered enough, and have a claim to be spared any further exactions: **they** will submit no longer to disagreeable necessity, for **they** are exceptions and intend to remain so.
> —Sigmund Freud

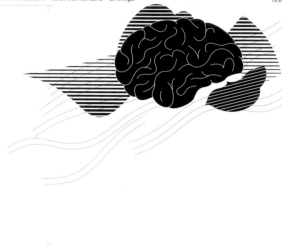

There exist, then, two sorts—two widely different species—of man. The first, of which I note countless specimens, evidently carries a head on its shoulders (and by "head" I mean a hairy eight-inch ball with various holes in it) while the second, of which I note only one specimen, evidently carries no such thing on its shoulders. And till now I had overlooked this considerable difference! Victim of a prolonged fit of madness, of a lifelong hallucination (and by "hallucination" I mean what my dictionary says: *apparent perception of an object not actually present*), I had invariably seen myself as pretty much like other men, and certainly never as a decapitated but still living biped. I had been blind to the one thing that is always present, and without which I am blind indeed—to this marvellous substitute-for-a-head, this unbounded clarity, this luminous and absolutely pure void, which nevertheless is—rather than contains— all things.

The Brain

11

"Time is fleeting, so take advantage

of every moment."

10

O plunge
your hands
in water,
Plunge them
in up to
the wrist:
Stare, stare
in the basin
you've
missed.

— W.H. Auden

25

strive

•••

While listening to the song by Hildegard von Bingen—

—rearrange or remove parts of these lines in any way without changing their shape or weight—

—adapt this shape by removing parts or sliding parts horizontally without losing the shape's identity—

—and integrate your icon image in a chosen size.

Later—

—reinterpret in color and link a specific text with the composition.

+ +   + **color and text**

118

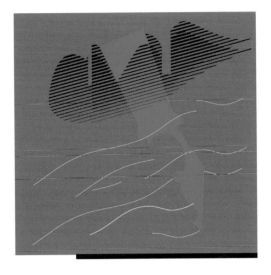

In the time before steamships, or then more frequently than now, a stroller along the docks of any considerable seaport would occasionally have his attention arrested by a group of bronzed mariners, man-o'-war's, men or merchant sailors in holiday attire, ashore on liberty.
— *Billy Budd, Sailor* by Herman Melville

What matters is

the successful

striving for what at

each moment

seems unattainable.

It is not the fruits

of that success

but the living in and

for the future in

which human

intelligence proves

itself.

Progress is move-

ment for movement's

sake, for it is

in the process of

learning, and in the

effects of having

learned something

new, that man

enjoys the gifts of his

intelligence.

Fredrick August
von Hayak

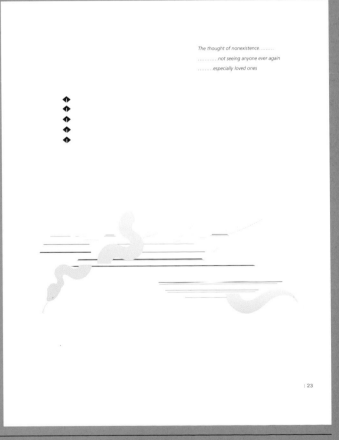

24

---

2 . 16 . 1770

"I shall hear in heaven."
Ludwig von Beethoven

The thought of nonexistence.........
............not seeing anyone ever again
.........especially loved ones

: 23

While listening to the Beethoven cello sonata selection—
—use the elements
and the process
described on the
facing page.

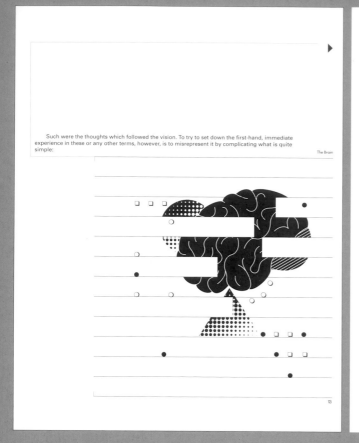

Such were the thoughts which followed the vision. To try to set down the first-hand, immediate experience in these or any other terms, however, is to misrepresent it by complicating what is quite simple:

The Brain

13

"Your colorful personality is the envy of all."

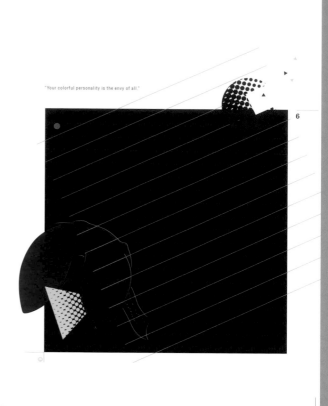

Enter
the Ghost of Caesar.

XXIV O murd'rous slumber!
Ha! who comes here? I
think it is the weakness of
mine eyes That shapes this
monstrous apparition.
It comes upon me.

Act IV Scene III

What in
me is dark
illumine,
what is low
raise and
support.

— John Milton

27

illuminate

While listening to Mickey Hart's "The Dancing Sorcerer"—

—use three of the four
rasterized elements below
and any number of the
small elements—

—work on a given
parallel line grid,
keeping all the lines—

—and integrate
your icon image in a
chosen size.

Later—
—reinterpret in color
and link a
specific text with the
composition.

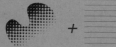 +  + **color and text**

By the road to the contagious hospital
under the surge of the blue
mottled clouds driven from the
northeast—a cold wind. Beyond, the
waste of broad, muddy fields
brown with dried weeds, standing and fallen

All along the road the reddish
purplish, forked, upstanding, twiggy
stuff of bushes and small trees
with dead, brown leaves under them
leafless vines—

They enter the new world naked,
cold, uncertain of all
save that they enter. All about them
the cold, familiar wind—

Spring and All

by
William Carlos Williams

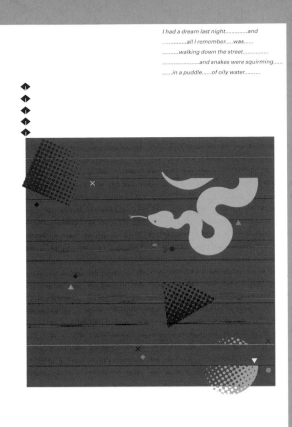

*I had a dream last night.............and
..............all I remember.....was......
.........walking down the street...............
......................and snakes were squirming......
......in a puddle......of oily water.........*

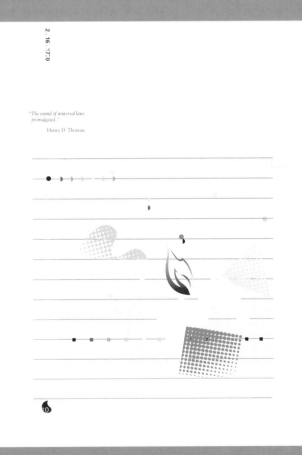

2 . 16 . '7:0

*"The sound of universal laws
promulgated."*

Henry D. Thoreau

While listening to John Lunn's *Echoes*—
—use the elements
and the process
described on the
facing page.

 +

For, however carefully I attend, I fail to find here even so much as a blank screen on which these mountains and sun and sky are projected, or a clear mirror in which they are reflected, or a transparent lens or aperture through which they are viewed—still less a soul or a mind to which they are presented, or a viewer (however shadowy) who is distinguishable from the view. Nothing whatever intervenes, not even that baffling and elusive obstacle called "distance": the huge blue sky, the pinkedged whiteness of the snows, the sparkling green of the grass— how can these be remote, when there's nothing to be remote from? The headless void here refuses all definition and location: it is not round, or small, or big, or even here as distinct from there. (And even if there were a head here to measure outwards from, the measuring-rod stretching from it to the peak of Everest would, when read end-on—arid there's no other way for me to read it—reduce to a point, to nothing.) In fact, these colored shapes present themselves in all simplicity, without any such complications as near or far, this or that, mine or not mine, seen-by-me or merely given. All twoness—all duality of subject and object— has vanished: it is no longer read into a situation which has no room for it.

The Brain

12

⑧

Deaf folk hear the fairies
However soft their song;
'Tis we who lose the honey sound
Amid the clamour all around
That beats the whole day long.

– Rose Fyleman

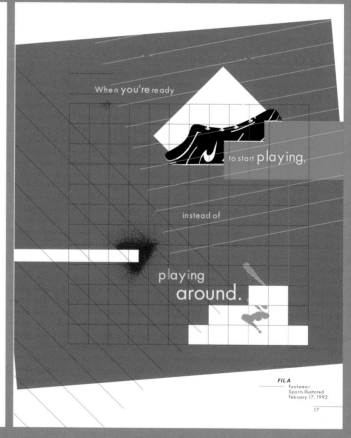

When you're ready

to start playing,

instead of

playing
around.

FILA
Footwear
Sports Illustrated
February 17, 1992

17

While listening to Arvo Pärt's *Tabula Rasa*—

—select two of these
three shapes—

—with your icon to
form a triad—

—and use the grid as a tool to enhance the
triadic relationship. Create "rests" from the
"ostinato" relentlessness of the grid by deletion.

Later—

—reinterpret in color;
link a specific text with
the composition.
Option: recycle parallel
lines from previous.

color and text

   +   + +

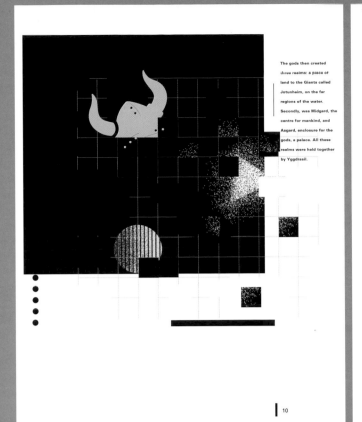

The gods then created three realms: a piece of land to the Giants called Jotunheim, on the far regions of the water. Secondly, was Midgard, the centre for mankind, and Asgard, enclosure for the gods, a palace. All these realms were held together by Yggdrasil.

10

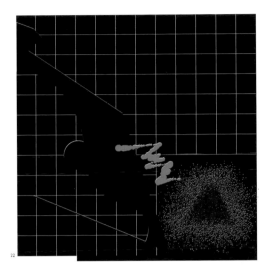

A merry little surge of electricity piped by automatic alarm from the mood organ beside his bed awakened Rick Deckard.
— *Blade Runner* by Philip K. Dick

22

The sources of her imagery lie in the world of N A T U R E but N A T U R E interpreted with great freedom, from precise realism to abstraction as pure as music.

Lloyd Goodrich

What is termed Sin is an essential element of progress. Without it the world would stagnate, or grow old, or become colourless. By its curiosity Sin increases the experience of the race. Through its intensified assertion of individualism, it saves us from monotony of type. In its rejection of the current notion about morality, it is one with the higher ethics.

Oscar Wilde

20

While listening to the opening segment of Arvo Pärt's "Miserere"—

—use the elements and the process described on the facing page.

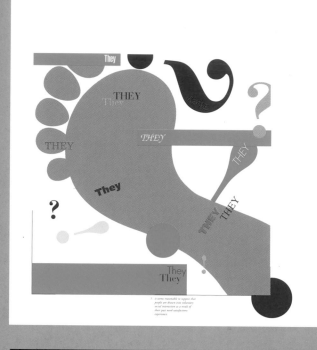

Since ever and ever the world began
They have danced like a ribbon of flame,
They have sung their song through the centuries long
And yet it is never the same.
And though you be foolish or though you be wise,
With hair of silver and gold,
You could never be young as the fairies are,
And never as old.

– Rose Fyleman

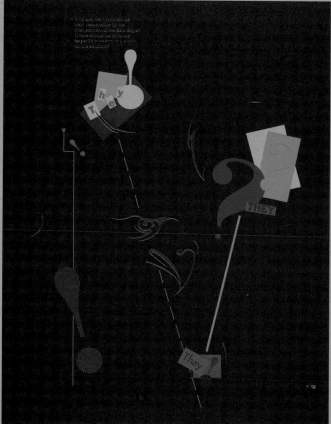

B l a m e

To place the

responsibility for

(a fault, error,

etc.) on

(a person)

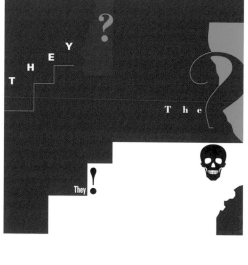

22

While listening to Harvey Goldman and Warren Lehrer's "They"—

—use any number of
THEYs in combination
with any number of
exclamation points
and question marks;

the type can reverse
out of shapes of any kind
and size—

—use lines as desired
to anchor the composition,
and integrate your
icon image in a chosen size.

Later—
—reinterpret in color
and link a
specific text with the
composition.

THEY **THEY** THEY *THEY* THEY **THEY** *THEY*
They **They** They They They **They** *They*

    color and text

they are of a brown and
pale green color intermixed
as if they were

• • • 17

They

?
They

THEY

THEY

?

They

?

watered with it

4.

Drawing from . . .

Personal Experience Mapping

Daily experience is a readily available, tangible—though seldom perceived—source for original form. Taking care of daily needs, routines, and social exchanges—no matter how ordinary—and characterizing these visually as a map presents an organic, systemic basis for constructing units, discrete segmentations, distinctions, boundaries.
This activity demands of the designer a language both personal and communicative.

In this chapter students are assigned experiences of the previous day as a given. A unique shape, intrinsic to the composite of experience, is developed in map form.

> *"The task of the designer*
> *is to give visual access to*
> *the subtle and the difficult—that is, the revelation*
> *of the complex."*
> —Edward R. Tufte

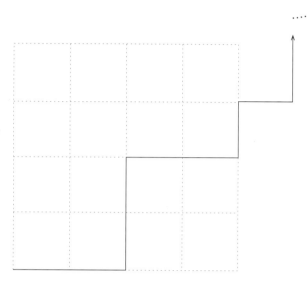

Wayfinding

In a broad sense all design involves mapping. The purpose of design is to present an image through which viewers can find their way. Whether one is designing a poster, a catalog, an instruction book, or an interactive multimedia piece, the essential goal is to clarify paths toward revelatory information.

Some maps are guides for future activity, others records of past action. There are personal maps of activities or projects that may be meaningful only to those who made them—a sort of "quick reference" to experience that function as memory props. Instructions for using products are too rarely seen as maps with starting points, landmarks, and destinations. Landmarks are lost in details. Steps easily become lost or redundant.

Many maps, such as music scores or architectural plans or road maps, must be readily comprehensible by others. These are denotative maps, where logical clarity has first priority. Connotative maps carry another level of meaning that is suggestive of qualities of a time, place, event, or subjectively experienced attributes while also performing their information-giving functions.

Whether a map is for personal use or for communication with others, creating a map is a good way to learn to use symbology and to develop logical sets of markings.

Identifying landmarks and placing them on a path as part of the system is the primary concern in map-making.

Paths and Sequence

In the most conventional sense, a path connects points. It is by this definition linear. The character or "color" of the line—its thickness, its degree and quality of fragmentation, whether it is curved or straight, light or dark, visible or invisible, whether it is simple or compounded, crude or refined—provides a base against which landmarks are contrasted. Paths are the means for understanding a sequence of places, events, or activities.

Process

1.
Note everything you can think of about the previous day:
places,
times,
durations,
events,
activities,
subject matter,
involvement level,
enjoyment level,
etc.

2.
Select two or three categories as emblematic of your day.

3.
Find a way to represent these symbolically, using essentially typographic forms. Limit yourself to either Garamond 3 or Times Roman, plus the Univers Family, Dingbats, and the abstract line/dot/pattern language available in a computer drawing program.

4.
Develop a language of landmarks and paths.

5.
Provide whatever text or key is required for communication.

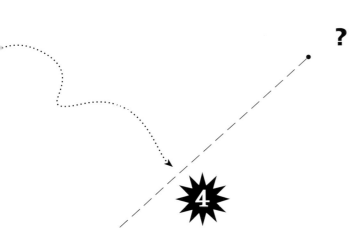

Landmarks

Landmarks typically are points. Landmarks are important to any communication. In this book, the chapter titles are landmarks, but each double-page spread has points of focus by which the eye gains its bearings. When giving directions to someone, it helps to name a business or other feature at a critical intersection, to transform the spot in the traveler's mind from a street corner like many others to one special street corner. In a geographical map, points are created by natural and human activity over time, the product of history. Our choices are limited to showing existing factual detail, such as towns, rivers, and highways, and in the degree of detail permissible. In connotative maps, landmarks can be developed in a more theme-specific and inventive way.

For a landmark to function well, it must be visually prominent and unique. Landmarks should be clear and reassuring points of orientation.

Symbols and Icons

A symbol is an abstract reference whose meaning is defined by a key. By contrast, an icon makes direct pictographic reference to the thing it represents. The purpose of using icons is to obviate the need for a key. However, compacting enough information into an icon to achieve this end also tends to complicate the image so that it may no longer be useful as a landmark.

Grids

An underlying structure is usually helpful in mapping. This provides a scale or other reference for the paths, landmarks, and other elements that belong to the surface structure. Because the underlying grid structure is usually latent, a neutral and simple pattern is most useful.

Sets and Supersets

Elements, whether paths, landmarks, or other marks, are grouped into sets, subsets, and super sets. Sets and hierarchically ordered subsets provide for the logical linkage of functionally related elements. These are the logical groupings that the eye picks up immediately. Supersets, which are created across the logical boundaries without confusing the logic, create a web of formal relation and interest. The cross-functioning of supersets is a means of "escaping flatland," of bringing depth into an otherwise linear or flat interpretation.

Keys and Mnemonic Value

Whether a map should be keyed within the map area or by a key placed outside its boundaries is one of the basic questions in using symbols. The further the explanation is from the symbol's appearance on the map, the greater the demand for reliable mnemonic (memory) reinforcement to avoid repeated and annoying reference to the key.

Sifts

Sifting out functional and formal sets is a way to test the viability of each kind of set.

The extensive pencil sketch and completion processes of one student are shown on pages 130–139. Pages 140–149 show sets and sifts in relation to end-product; pages 150–152 show additional end-products.

Goals

6.
Organize the presentation of this introduction and your map work into a given publication grid. (Pages 136–137 of this chapter are examples of this phase.) Test your system by designing a second spread with the map project furnished by another student.

—to exercise the memory of experience

—to combine denotative and connotative aspects of experience in a diagram

—to compare verbal description with visual notation

—to symbolize the parts of an experience

—to organize an experience logically

—to codify aspects of judgment and subjectivity

—to develop a clarity of image that can absorb varying levels of complexity and that is retained and

enhanced by the application of a color idea

—to integrate a resulting map design into another format with additional information requirements

—to hone manual and computer drawing skills

Evolution of a map

The series of pencil sketches on pages 130–135 was achieved during four studio sessions a week apart. Pencil is an ideal tool for exploring approaches:

• erasing and revision are easy and direct.

• the sketches can easily be displayed for comparison and to see which directions yield greatest clarity and interest.

• the process is personal, depending on touch and immediate response.

• a valuable rhythm of alternation between hand and machine processes is furthered.

After choosing a specific direction, drawing using a computer program begins.

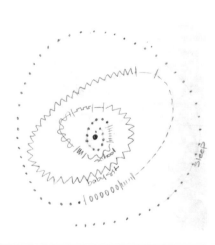

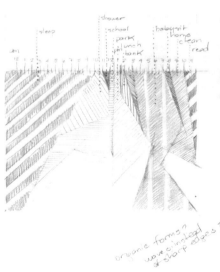

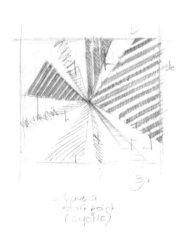

1

Key idea 1.
Activities are placed on a single trajectory of varied line quality. The overall movement is from the nebulous realm of sleep to focused activity.

2–4

Key idea 2.
Activities are graphed on a straight timeline and assigned a value. The exploration progresses from relatively neutral bars to articulated ones.

5

Key idea 3.
Activities radiate from a center, varying in strength (weight) and duration (width of wedge).

130

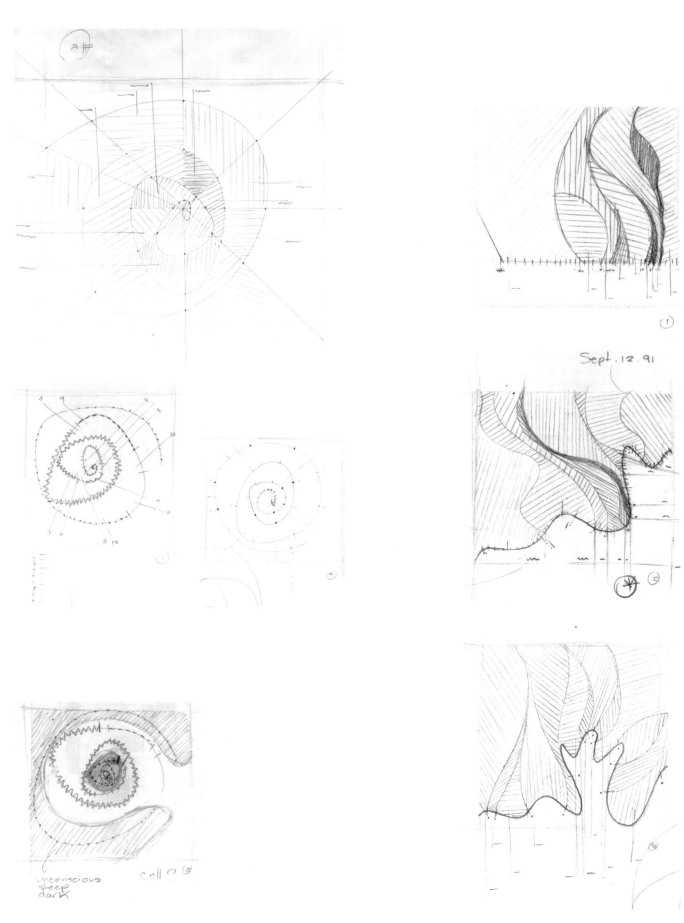

Sept.12.91

unconscious
sleep
dark

cell

6–9

Key idea 1 is explored,
applying more precise
notations of time intervals
and a more expressive
overall impact.

10–12

Key idea 2 is explored,
differentiating both
the timeline and the activity
zones to reflect differences
without being specific about
qualities.

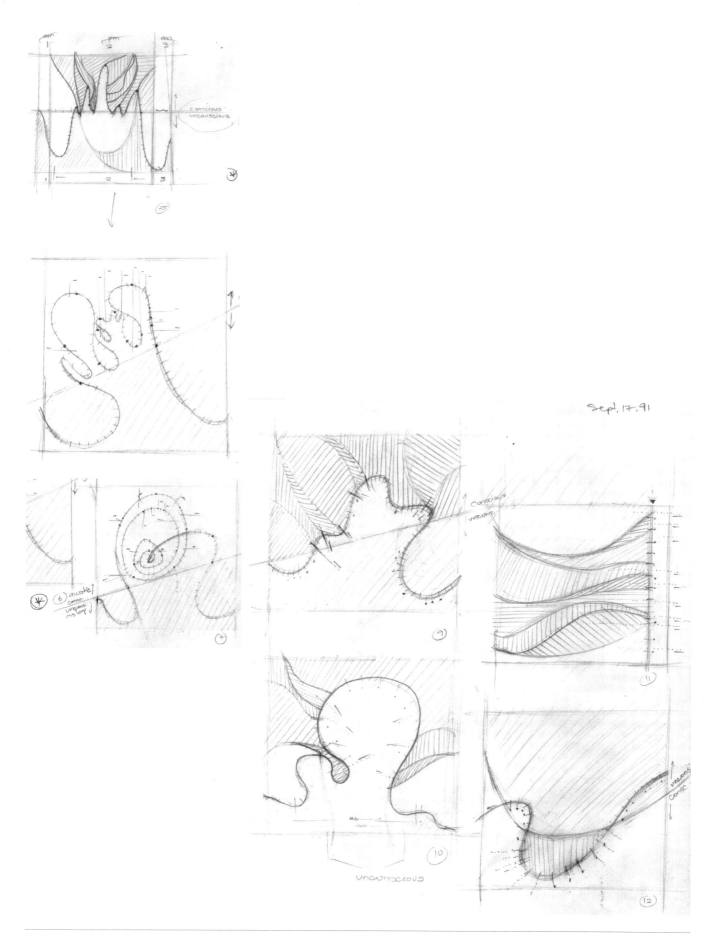

Sept. 17, 91

132

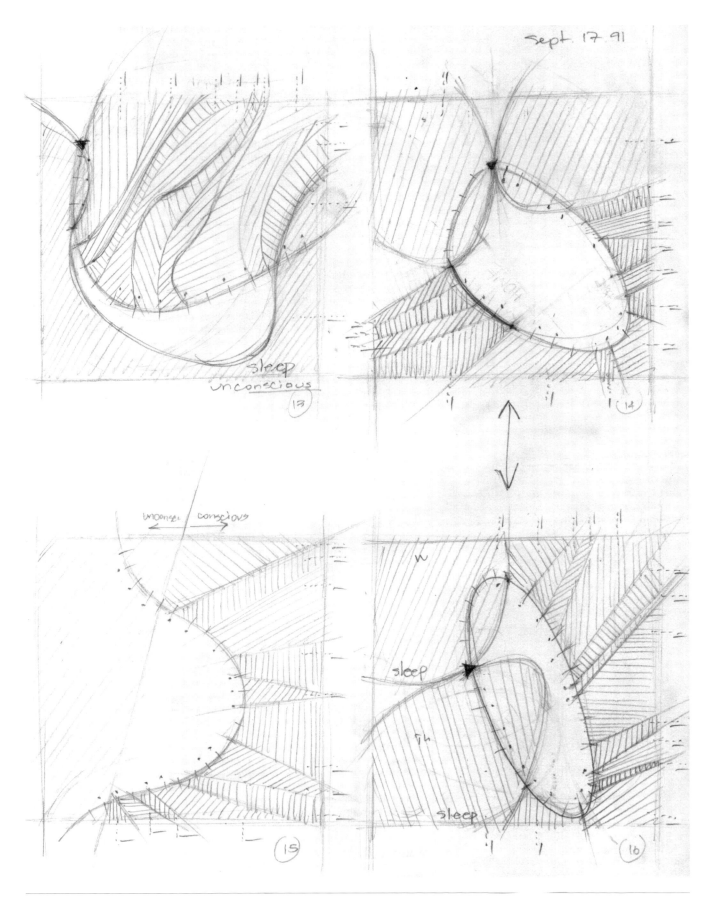

sept. 17. 91

sleep
unconscious
⑬

⑭

unconscious ← → conscious

sleep

sleep

⑮

⑯

Through exploration an
ellipse is defined as the
center, introducing key idea
3. Different activities are as
yet aesthetically, not
functionally, contrasted.

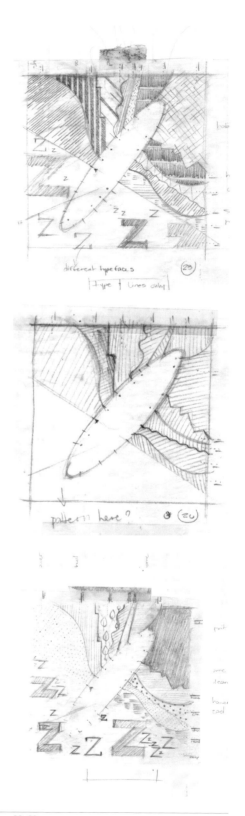

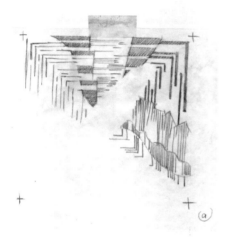

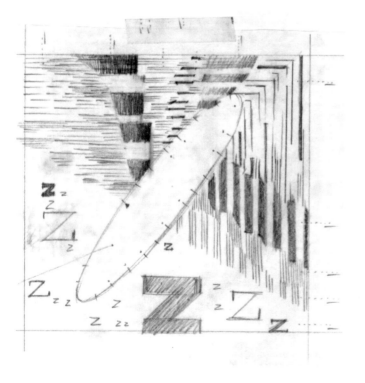

24-25

Experiments in assigning
specific qualities to specific
activities using a rectilinear
base matrix.

26–28

Experiments in assigning
specific qualities to specific
activities using a curvilinear
base matrix.

134

Finding form to match meaning:

In this student's words, "Everything relates to the sleep zone (my personal twilight zone). Each activity of the day is enclosed in one shape. The pleasant ones open up, the not-so-pleasant ones close. The random lines mean that I was home. The even-spaced ones mean that I was out, engaged in each one of the different activities. The weights of the lines on each section signify the subjective value of the experience and the amount of activity."

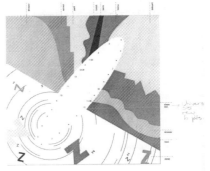

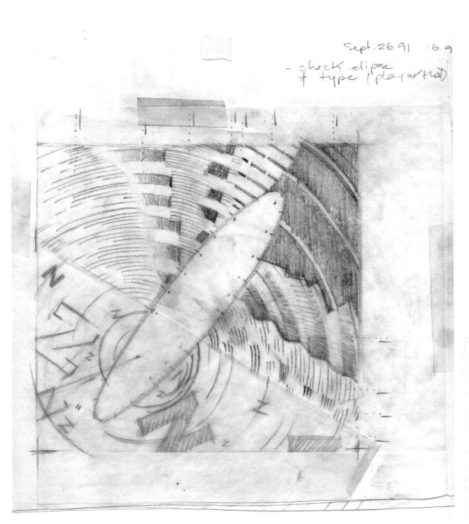

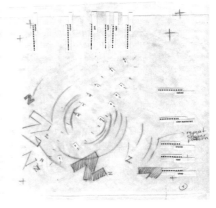

29 ▶

The shape of the experience zones is clarified to allow concentration on the textural contrast between them and on the integration of an underlying concentric ring matrix.

30

The organization of the zones of experience against a concentric ring matrix increases the image complexity and depth while unifying it.

31–34

Development of detail using manual cut-and-paste techniques.

mapping ▶ **135**

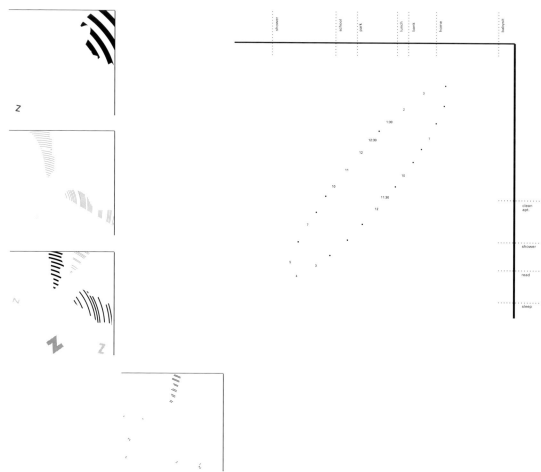

35–40

*A selection of sifts
according to relatedness of
line quality and weight.
The clarity of each subset
contributes to the clarity
of the whole.*

Verbal description.
The twenty-four-hour
clock. It was my
first day back in the
States after a long
vacation at my home
in South America. I
was still sleepy and
tired and to some
degree unaware of the
activities of the
day. I was really
happy to be back in
my apartment and
especially to stop by
school and see my
friends. The visit to
the bank was not
pleasant at all, since

I found out my
financial status at the
moment—I was
absolutely broke.
Babysitting was fun
but also tiring.
The whole day was
like sleepwalking.
Finally I got home
and relaxed a bit
before cleaning up.
Then I took a
wonderful shower,
read for a while, and
at last succumbed to
a great deep sleep.

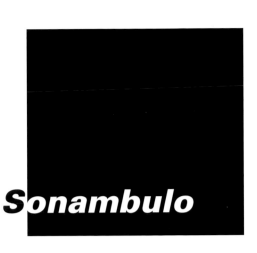

Sonambulo

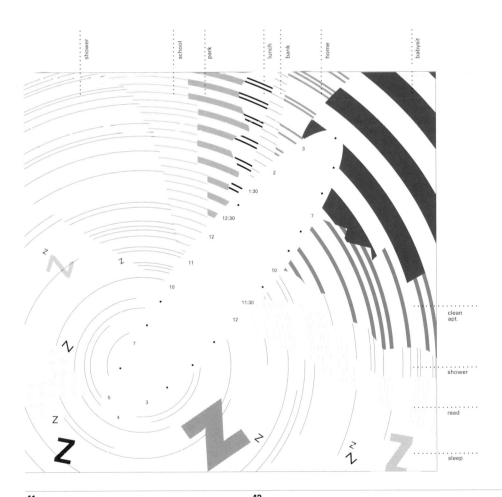

41

*The student's verbal
description shows the
difference between verbal
and visual modes. Each
requires a measure of
imagination for completion:
the verbal requires
imagination of the visual;*
*the visual requires transla-
tion to words, but
engages the mind more
immediately.*

42

*The composite map as
drawn in a computer
program before the addition
of color. Curvilinear shapes
represent pleasurable
activities; angular ones, less
so.*

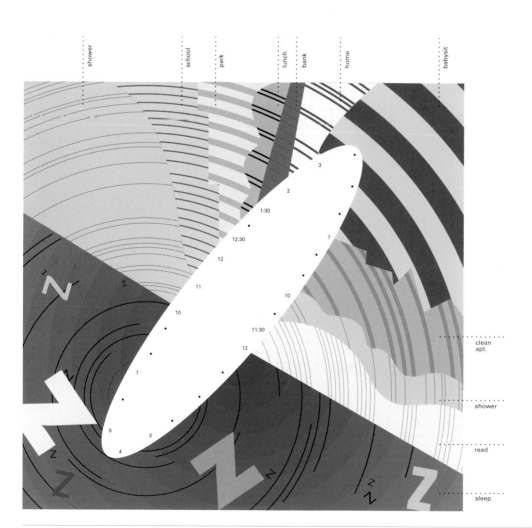

shower

school

park

lunch

bank

home

babysit

3

2

1:30

12:30

12

7

11

10

10

11:30

clean
apt.

12

7

shower

5

3

read

4

sleep

43

*An overall warm-cool
color contrast defines
daytime compared to night.
Color changes during
daytime are a reflection of
the relative "noisiness"
of the activities.*

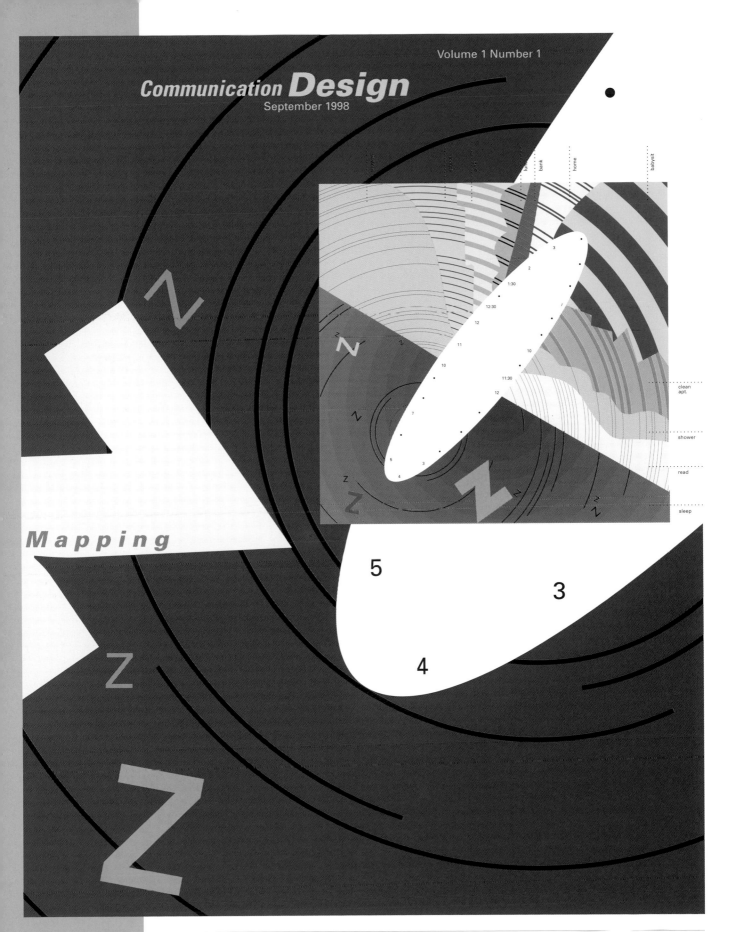

Communication Design
September 1998

Volume 1 Number 1

Mapping

Extension. This application of the map in a magazine cover expands the environment and the potential for another layer of interest and dynamic action. It enlivens the completion of an extended process with a new impetus provided by a pragmatic requirement.

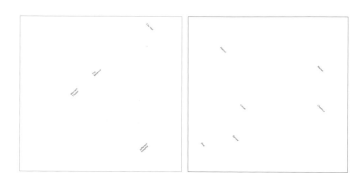

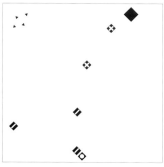

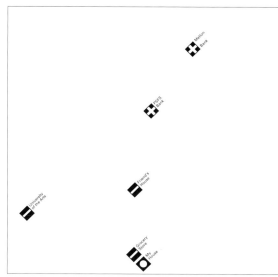

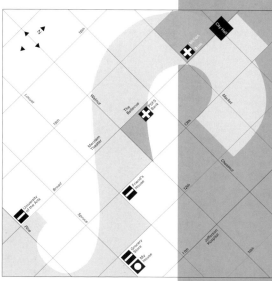

Theme:
"Money In, Money Out"

A set of transactions in different places is characterized by + and – signs, giving them a key archetypal significance. The sifts of functional sets show formal rhythmic and functional clarity.

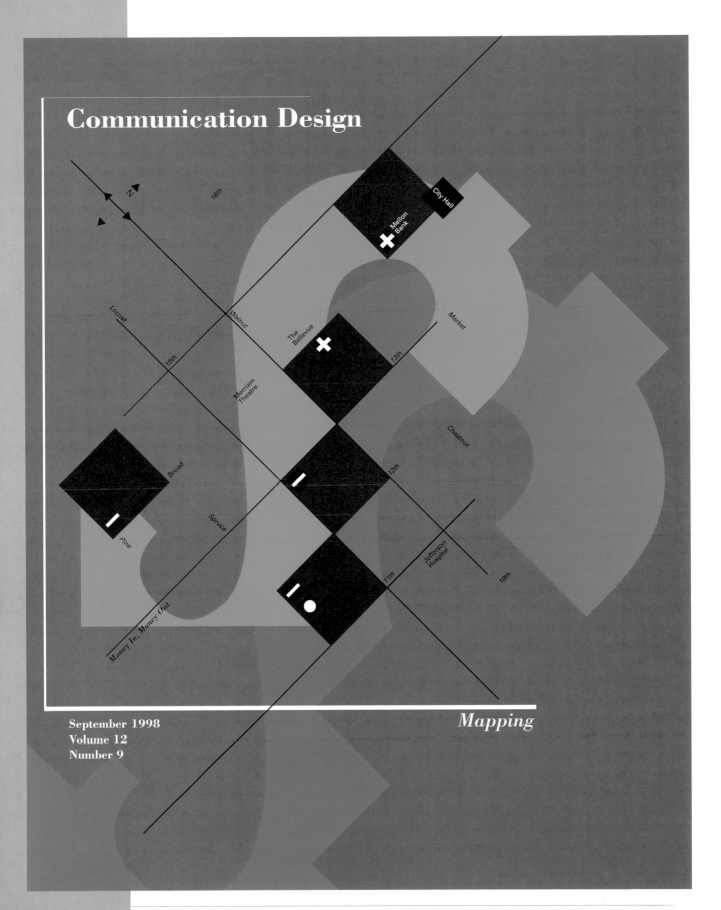

Communication Design

September 1998
Volume 12
Number 9

Mapping

Adaptation to a new format
forces decisions to edit
the grid lines to a more
essential and rhythmic level
and to find a color logic.
Casting the dollar sign as
having both a bright quality
and a dark one reinforces
the +/– theme.

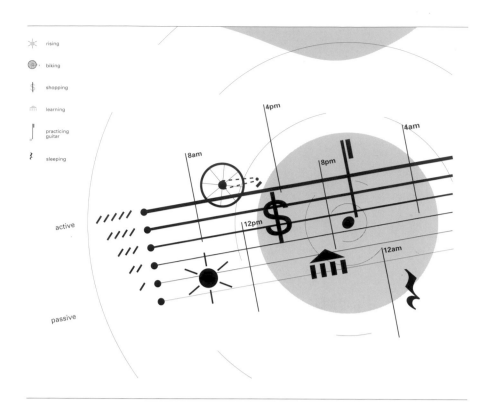

rising

biking

shopping

learning

practicing
guitar

sleeping

active

passive

4pm

4am

8am

8pm

$

12pm

12am

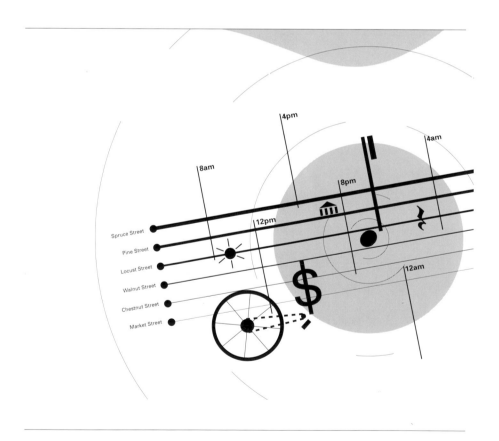

4pm

4am

8am

8pm

Spruce Street

12pm

Pine Street

Locust Street

$

Walnut Street

Chestnut Street

12am

Market Street

Theme:
"Toning"

"The day begins at eight
o'clock in the morning. The
fitness program that follows
began at ten-thirty. The next
activity, shopping, began
at one o'clock in the
afternoon. Class began at
seven in the evening.
Practicing the guitar brought
an end to the day."

Version 1 (top):
The icons are all the same
size. Their placement on a
scale from passive to active
shows the mapmaker's
degree of involvement in
the activities.

Version 2 (bottom):
The icons are placed on a
grid to indicate where
activities took place. The
change of size indicates
the degree of involvement.
The display combines
more features and achieves
greater clarity than
version 1.

Communication **Design**

September 1999
Volume 45 Number 9

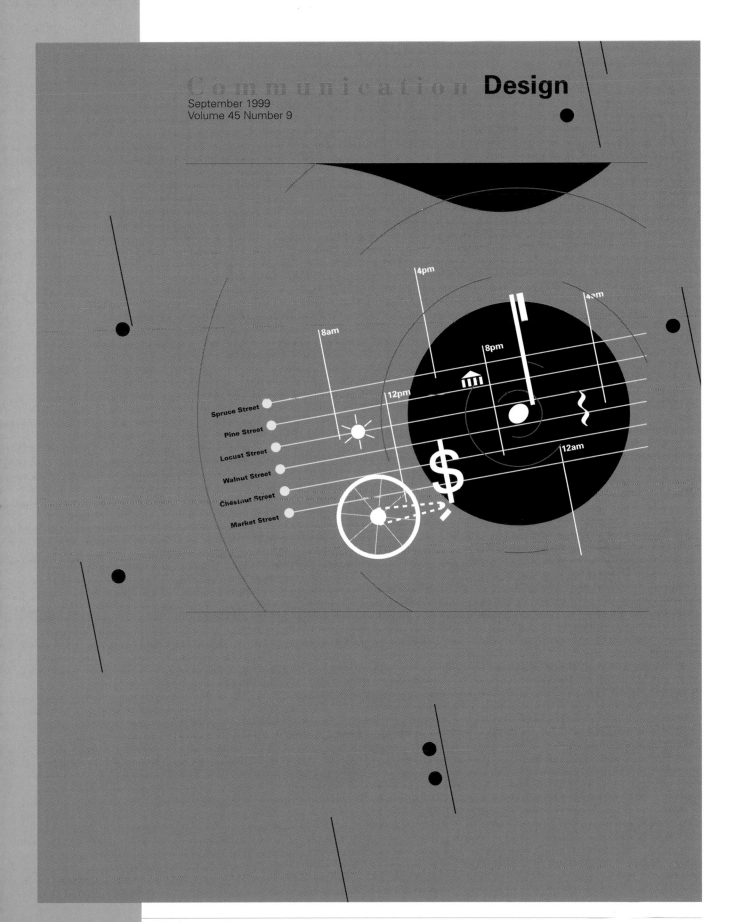

Adaptation to a new format
allows the musical refer-
ence of the final activity of
the day to expand. Light and
dark and color are used to
separate night and day
activities. The suggestion of
a guitar form supported by
color adds to the meaning.

1

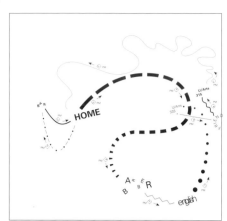

4

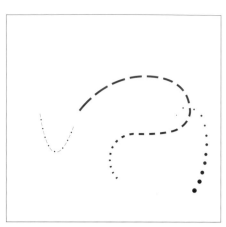

2

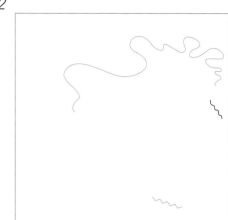

5

3

6

**Theme:
"Winding Through the
Day"**

"I open my eyes and realize
that I am back in
Philadelphia. At this moment
I know that my vacation is
over, but I do not have any
class until late in the
afternoon. I have the rest of
the morning and part of the
afternoon for myself.
The first thing I do is go to
the bathroom, and I realize

that I need a haircut. I leave
home for the barber, and
my day out on the street is
beginning. I experience
all the different paths that I
take during the day with
different emotional states.
These states change
depending on time, place,
and destination."

The sifts show:
1. all elements
2. wiggly solid path
elements—negative
impulses
3. experience of places
interpreted typographically

4. dotted path elements
connote spontaneous flow
5. simple solid path
elements—determined
action
6. time markings combined
with path direction signals.

September 1997
Volume 32
Number 5

Communication Design

mapping

Adaptation to a new format
in color allows reinforcement of the emotional tenor
of the path with hot and
cold color. Highlighting the
time icons gives them a
desirable prominence.

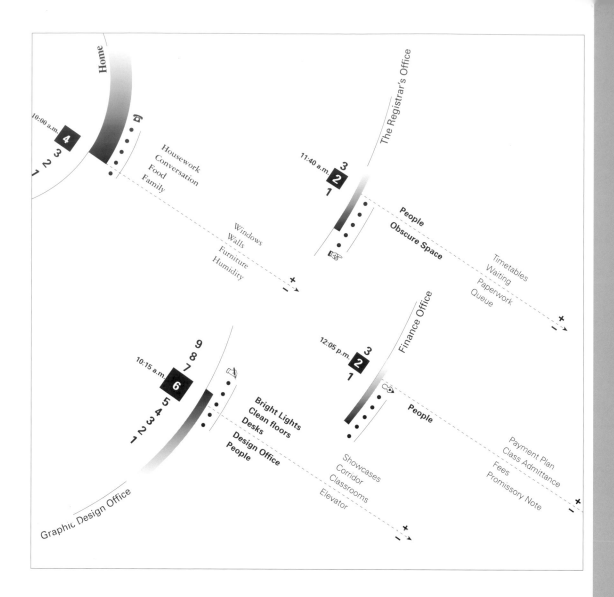

Home

10:00 a.m.

4
3
2
1

Housework
Conversation
Food
Family

Windows
Walls
Furniture
Humidity

+
−

The Registrar's Office

11:40 a.m.

3
2
1

People

Obscure Space

Timetables
Waiting
Paperwork
Queue

+
−

9
8
7

10:15 a.m.

6

5
4
3
2
1

Bright Lights
Clean floors
Desks

Design Office
People

Graphic Design Office

Showcases
Corridor
Classrooms

Elevator

+
−

Finance Office

12:05 p.m.

3
2
1

People

Payment Plan
Class Admittance
Fees
Promissory Note

+
−

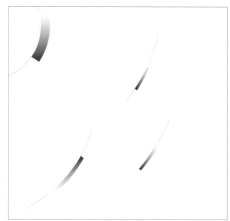

Theme:
"Up and Down"

This approach deals with a
sequence of four experi-
ences in terms of levels—
physically as the number of
floors up from ground
and psychologically as
positive or negative
experiences. Each experi-
ence is characterized by an
armature against which
movement occurs.

The sifts show the basic
contrast of arcs emanating
from home and the
diagonal flow of information
on a +/- axis.

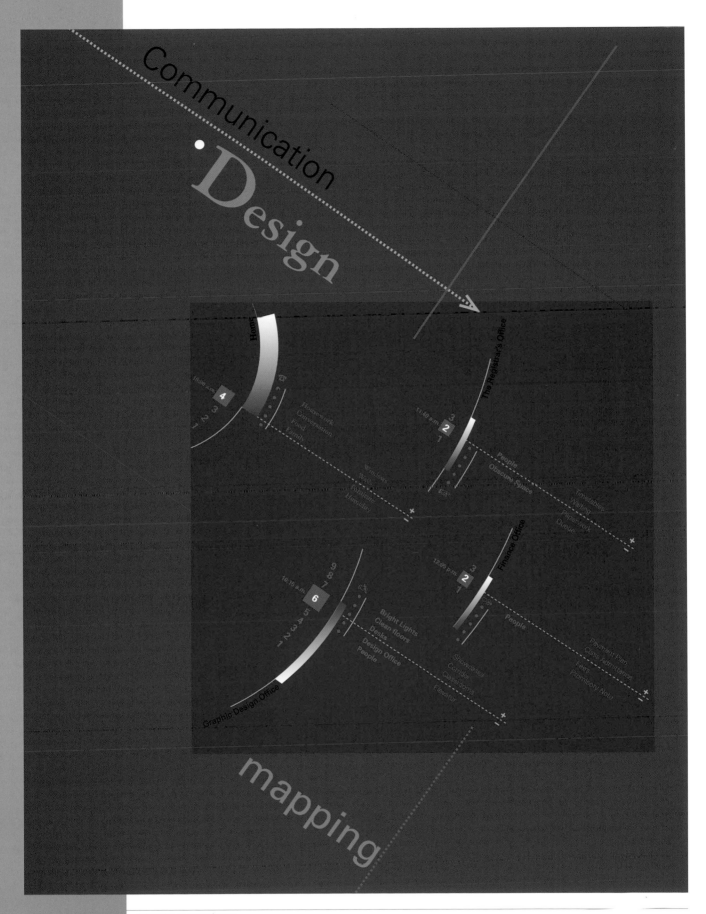

Communication

Design

mapping

Adaptation to a new format in color emphasizes the emotional content of the information.

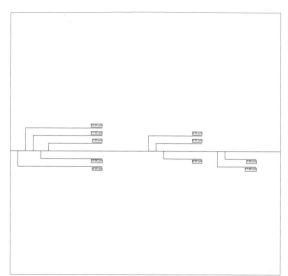

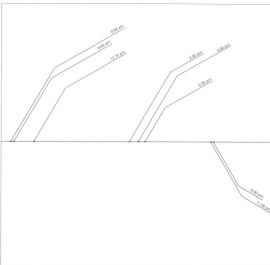

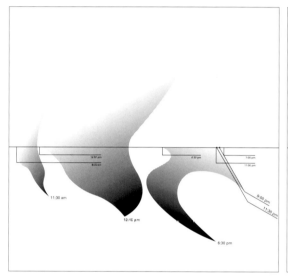

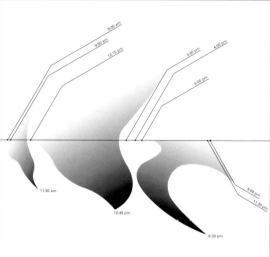

**Theme:
"The Unexpected:
Pleasant"**

*This approach contrasts
times of the events planned
in a day's schedule (right
angle lines) with actual
times (diagonal lines) and
combines this information
with the totally unexpected
and pleasant (free-formed
solids). The horizon line
divides practical matters
(above) from social activities
(below).*

Communication
DESIGN

Special Issue:
Mapping

September 1998
Volume 39, Number 4

*Adaptation to a new format
in color transforms the
graphlike information into an
exuberant statement
within which the tedious
is a minor rhythm.*

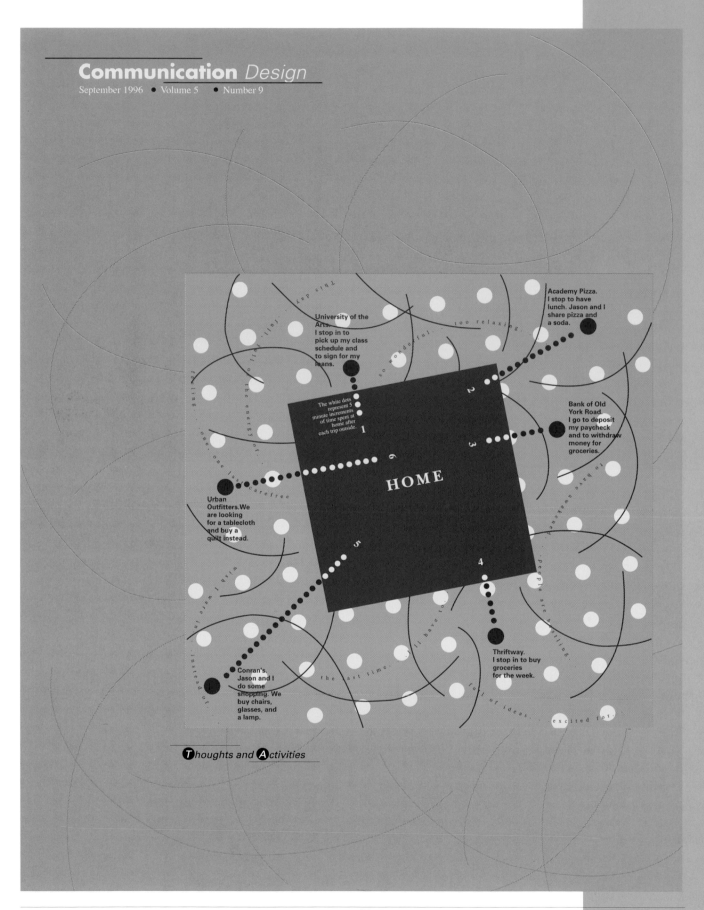

University of the
Arts.
I stop in to
pick up my class
schedule and
to sign for my
loans.

Academy Pizza.
I stop to have
lunch. Jason and I
share pizza and
a soda.

The white dots
represent 5
minute increments
of time spent at
home after
each trip outside.

Bank of Old
York Road.
I go to deposit
my paycheck
and to withdraw
money for
groceries.

HOME

Urban
Outfitters. We
are looking
for a tablecloth
and buy a
quilt instead.

Conran's.
Jason and I
do some
shopping. We
buy chairs,
glasses, and
a lamp.

Thriftway.
I stop in to buy
groceries
for the week.

Thoughts and **A**ctivities

Theme:
"Thoughts and Activities"

Color is a means to
heighten the layers
of information and convey
the bright quality of the day,
especially its warm center.

Volume 4
Number 5

communication design

September 1995
Special Issue: Mapping

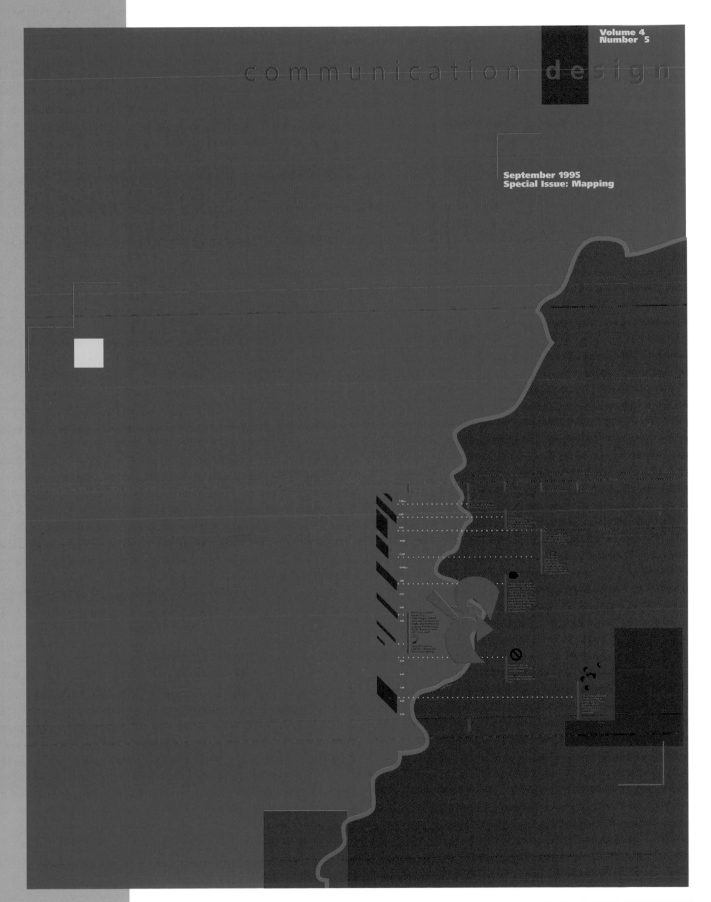

Theme:
"The Near Miss"

Events are located accord
ing to place (x coordinate)
and time (y coordinate).
A simplified map gives a
concrete geographical
context for the near-
catastrophe on the road.
The map of a person's
day is cast in a larger
perspective by radical scale
change.

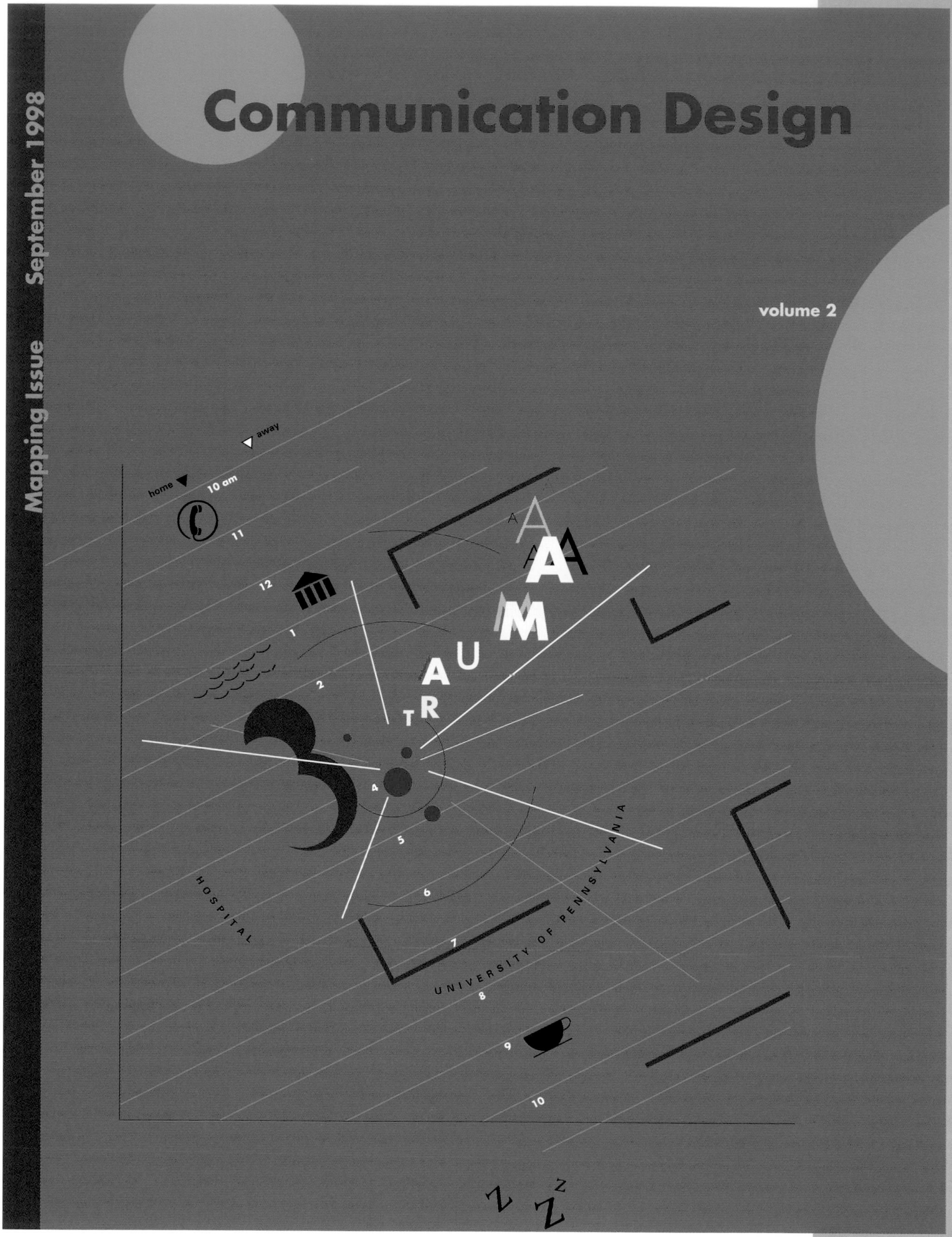

Communication Design

volume 2

home ▼   10 am
away ▽
11
12
1
2
3
4
5
6
7
8
9
10

TRAUMA

HOSPITAL

UNIVERSITY OF PENNSYLVANIA

Z Z Z

Theme:
"Flying Bullets"

The map by an ER nurse places events on a time path, dividing between events at home and away. Routine events are contrasted with a dominant experience treating gun-shot wounds.

5.

Drawing from . . .

Statistical Data

Numeric relationships treated vividly can either mislead or
enhance understanding.

In this chapter pure statistical data,
displayed in a neutral tabular format with
a criterion of maximum objectivity, is
the basis for progressively more revealing
and cogent dramatizations of data without distortion or falsification.

> *"Everyone spoke of an information overload, but what there was in fact was a non-information overload."*
>
> —Richard Saul Wurman

Although all design is based on information, working with statistical information presents special challenges. For one thing, many people find statistics eminently boring. They resent the idea that things, attitudes, points of view, and choices can be reduced to numbers. They view numbers as cold, cerebral, resisting the poetic, and resisting depth of experience.

Yet there is more to numerical relationships than this. They are the basis for many religious mysteries and are often assigned emotional qualities. Numerical relationships underlie music. The key word here is *relationships*. When rightly conveyed, statistical information places data in a context that truly enlightens. If the context is rich, the deciphering process may not be instantaneous, as some would expect with statistical data as compared to prose description. In such cases it may take longer to grasp the meaning, but the reward of having comprehended context and possible ramifications can be correspondingly great. And when the task of processing information aids in remembering it—when it has a mnemonic value—there is an additional gain.

This chapter relies heavily on the information concerning set theory and mapping described in chapter 4. The informational base in this chapter is objective, chosen from available data.

Remember that information in and of itself is powerful. Like newspaper headlines, "data graphics" can be meaningful encapsulations. If badly designed, without proper interpretation and an identifying viewpoint, data graphics, like headlines, can easily be the source for erroneous deductions.

Information represented statistically is usually believed to be factual, but this is not necessarily so. If it appears to be true, it may be received as true even when it isn't.

Criteria for Effective Data Graphics

These principles and criteria are condensed in part from Edward R. Tufte's *The Visual Display of Quantitative Information*. They give a succinct summary of the goals for what Tufte calls "data graphics."

Graphic displays of data should:
— serve a reasonably clear purpose: description, comparison, contextualization;
— show the data;
— cause the viewer to think about what the data mean rather than how the display was made;
— avoid distorting what the data have to say;
— encourage the eye to compare different pieces of data;
— reveal the data at several levels of detail, from fine structure to broad overview;
— be closely integrated with the statistical base of the data and the verbal descriptions, including the title, of the display;
— not confuse design variation with data variation;
— not show more information-carrying dimensions than the number of dimensions in the data;
— assist in remembering the information; and
— respect the viewer's intelligence.

Principles of Graphical Integrity:

1. Proportional correspondence.
The representation of numbers, as physically measured on the surface of the graphic display, should be directly proportional to the numerical quantities represented.

2. Data-ink proportionality.
The largest share of ink should be used to show measured quantities (as compared to ink used for the measurement system).

3. Clear labeling.
Data need clear, detailed, and thorough labeling to eliminate graphical distortion and ambiguity. Write explanations of the data on the graphic. Label important events in the data.

4. Contextual relevance.
If you do not furnish the context, the viewer will. (If something goes up, something related goes down, etc.)

5. Device relevance.
Suppress vibrations, grids, self-promoting graphics, and expression of data by the use of relevant graphic devices, typographic manipulation, and finesse in the relative weighting of elements.

6. Shape relevance.
Information should not be squeezed into forms that deny its characteristic shape. Being true to information yields its own new form.

Note concerning the displays: ➤

Each spread shows several stages of students' process beginning with the base table. These tables are reproduced at reduced scale but should be sufficiently legible to give the background information for the larger-scale data-graphics shown on the righthand pages.

When you read this chapter, the tables used as a base will be out of date. This should not detract from the validity of the process.

Project Goals:

—To develop fluency
- in evaluating the validity of data comparisons
- in the typographic structuring of data for maximum clarity
- in the potential for expression of a given data set through typo graphic variation and augmentation
- in the composition of data structures using a computer page-layout program.

—To satisfy the criteria for clear data graphics.

—To understand limitations of visual information display.

Process:

1.
Choose a Worldwatch Paper topic from the options furnished. Select from the paper two sets of tabular data that you feel succinctly express the dilemma of social or environmental concern of your topic. One subject will be chosen after discussion.

2.
Convert this table using 9 point Garamond 3 typeface without any capital letters, boldface, or italic emphases. The success of this presentation of the data depends entirely on the use of space and placement to clarify the hierarchical and set structure as clear visual rhythms. Cohesiveness and consistency of alignments are necessary. Sketches for this phase are to be done in pencil.

3.
Set up a tabular structure on a master page using tabs in a computer page layout program. The external format size is 5.5" x 8.5" vertical or horizontal.

4.
In a series of manipulations, add simple graphic elements (rule lines, shapes, or other typographic elements) to emphasize the structure, highlight key elements, or sift out a group of elements. The criterion for these additions is that the legibility and accessibility of the data are heightened without distortion. Avoid chartjunk—extraneous elements added purely for interest but distracting to the data. Make at least 10 variations. Then make changes of typeface and size to achieve the same goal.

5.
Use the language of geometry to assign visual value to selected sets of information. Decide by experimentation how much information can be clearly communicated visually before excessive density detracts.

6.
Add color to support the data.

1.
Base

2.
Gradients used to show expected proportional reduction in costs of separate renewable energy sources.

3.
The line graph isolates the predicted overtaking of fossil fuel costs by photovoltaics in an immediate and precise comparison.

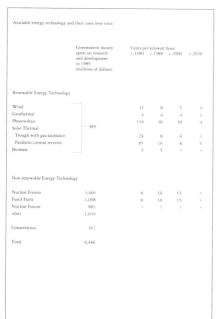

Available energy technology and their costs over time.

	Government money spent on research and development in 1989 (millions of dollars)	Cents per kilowatt hour c.1980 c.1988 c.2000 c.2030

Renewable Energy Technology

		c.1980	c.1988	c.2000	c.2030
Wind		32	8	5	5
Geothermal		4	4	4	5
Photovoltaic		339	30	10	4
Solar Thermal	489				
Trough with gas assistance		24	8	6	?
Parabolic/central receiver		85	16	8	5
Biomass		5	5	?	?

Non-renewable Energy Technology

Nuclear Fission	3,466	8	10	15	?
Fossil Fuels	1,098	8	10	15	?
Nuclear Fusion	883	?	?	?	?
other	1,039				
Conservation	367				
Total	6,486				

Available energy technology and their costs over time.

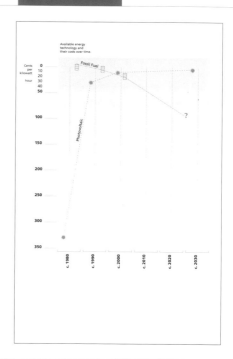

1.
Base

2.
The outer ring represents 100% of the landmass and population. The indigenous population and per capita area are shown as relative proportions.

1992 Estimated Populations of Indigenous People Compared to Areas Legally Controlled

country	total population (x millions)	share of national population (percent)	total land area (x 1,000 sq km)	share of national territory (percent)	area per capita (sq km)
Papua New Guinea	3.6	77	462	97	.15
Ecuador	10.8	38	269	41	.05
Mexico	82.7	12	1,958	8	.01
New Zealand	3.3	12	268	6	.04
Canada	26.5	4	9,971	22	2.46
Australia	17.1	2	7,683	12	2.23
Brazil	144.3	1	8,512	7	.38
USA	249.0	1	9,529	4	.18

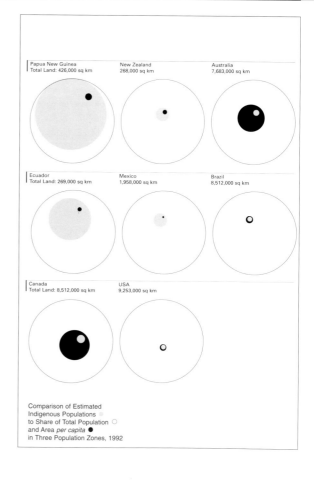

Comparison of Estimated Indigenous Populations to Share of Total Population and Area *per capita* in Three Population Zones, 1992

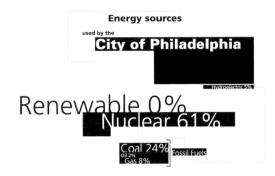

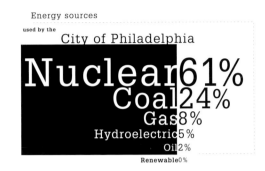

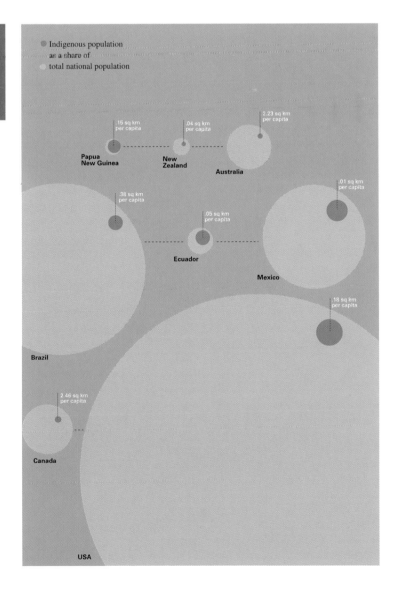

1. Base

2. The progression gives an immediate general indication of the change in the figures of the last and crucial column.

3. Accenting these countries places them in sharp contrast to the others.

Armed Forces and Employment
in Military Industry

Country	Military Industry Employees (thousand)	Armed Forces (thousand)	Total	Military Industry as Share of Industrial Employment
Israel	90	180	270	27.7
United States	3,350	2,212	5,562	14.4
Soviet Union	4,800	3,393	8,793	12.6
China	5,000	3,530	8,530	10.0
United Kingdom	620	328	948	9.8
France	300	559	859	5.6
Egypt	100	450	550	5.5
Poland	260	441	701	5.2
Canada	89	86	175	3.9
Belgium	33	109	142	3.7

Armed Forces and Employment
in Military Industry

Country	Military Industry Employees (thousand)	Armed Forces (thousand)	Total	Military Industry as Share of Industrial Employment
Israel	90	180	270	27.7
United States	3,350	2,212	5,562	14.4
Soviet Union	4,800	3,393	8,793	12.6
China	5,000	3,530	8,530	10.0
United Kingdom	620	328	948	9.8
France	300	559	859	5.6
Egypt	100	450	550	5.5
Poland	260	441	701	5.2
Canada	89	86	175	3.9
Belgium	33	109	142	3.7

Armed Forces and Employment
in Military Industry

Country	Military Industry Employees (thousand)	Armed Forces (thousand)	Total	Military Industry as Share of Industrial Employment
Israel	90	180	270	27.7
United States	3,350	2,212	5,562	14.4
Soviet Union	4,800	3,393	8,793	12.6
China	5,000	3,530	8,530	10.0
United Kingdom	620	328	948	9.8
France	300	559	859	5.6
Egypt	100	450	550	5.5
Poland	260	441	701	5.2
Canada	89	86	175	3.9
Belgium	33	109	142	3.7

1. Base

2. Tracking two selected cities in the base table clarifies their convergence as well as the shift in position of the other cities.

The World's Ten Most Populated Metropolitan Areas
(Population in millions)

2000¹

Mexico City	25.6
Sao Paulo	22.1
Tokyo	19.0
Shanghai	17.0
New York	16.8
Calcutta	15.7
Bombay	15.4
Beijing	14.0
Los Angeles	13.9
Jakarta	13.7

1980

Tokyo	16.9
New York	15.6
Mexico City	14.5
Sao Paulo	12.2
Shanghai	11.7
Buenos Aires	9.9
Los Angeles	9.5
Calcutta	9.0
Beijing	9.0
Rio de Janeiro	8.8

1950

New York	12.3
London	10.4
Tokyo	6.7
Paris	5.4
Shanghai	5.3
Buenos Aires	5.0
Chicago	4.9
Moscow	4.8
Calcutta	4.4
Los Angeles	4.0

¹Projections

The World's Ten Most Populated Metropolitan Areas
Showing Tracking of Two Selected Cities
(Population in millions)

2000¹

Mexico City	25.6
Sao Paulo	22.1
Tokyo	19.0
Shanghai	17.0
New York	16.8
Calcutta	15.7
Bombay	15.4
Beijing	14.0
Los Angeles	13.9
Jakarta	13.7

1980

Tokyo	16.9
New York	15.6
Mexico City	14.5
Sao Paulo	12.2
Shanghai	11.7
Buenos Aires	9.9
Los Angeles	9.5
Calcutta	9.0
Beijing	9.0
Rio de Janeiro	8.8

1950

New York	12.3
London	10.4
Tokyo	6.7
Paris	5.4
Shanghai	5.3
Buenos Aires	5.0
Chicago	4.9
Moscow	4.8
Calcutta	4.4
Los Angeles	4.0

¹Projections

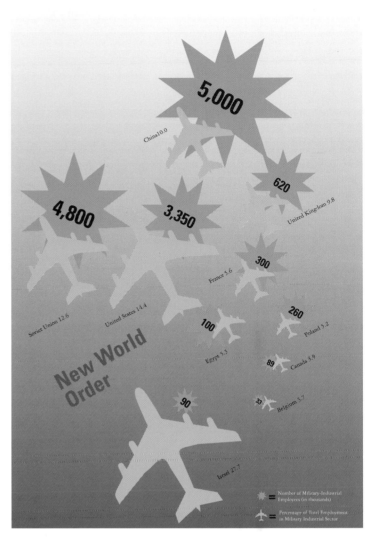

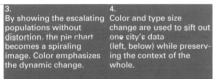

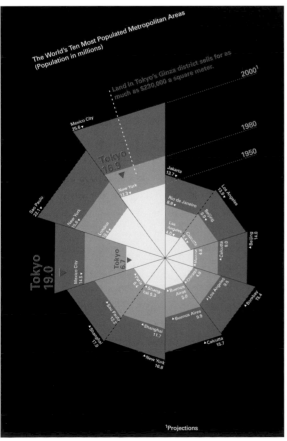

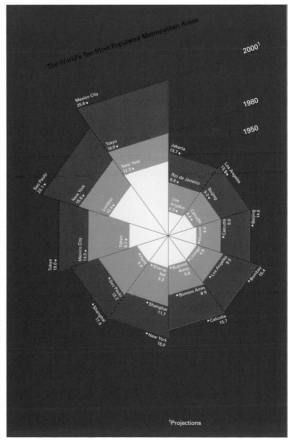

Labor, capital, and energy requirements and pollution produced by manufacturing U.S. 1987/88

industries	Inputs needed to generate $1,000 of value–added			GDP	employment	energy use	toxic release
	labor	capital	energy				
	hours	$ of assets	million BTUs	% of all manufacturing			
chemicals	8	1,039	22.4	9.0	5.5	21.2	58.4
paper	19	1,448	36.7	4.6	3.6	11.5	13.6
primary metal	24	1,581	45.9	4.3	4.0	14.0	12.5
refining & coal products	9	2,670	127.0	3.9	.8	31.2	3.7
transportation equipment	18	649	2.4	5.8	10.6	1.7	1.6
food products	17	665	7.6	8.7	8.4	4.8	1.4
electric machinery	20	695	2.2	10.0	10.7	1.1	1.4
non–electric machinery	20	677	2.0	9.5	10.7	1.4	.4
lumber & wood products	40	805	13.0	3.2	3.9	2.0	.2

Labor, capital, and energy requirements and pollution produced by manufacturing U.S. 1987/88

industries	Inputs needed to generate $1,000 of value–added			GDP	employment	energy use	toxic release
	labor	capital	energy				
	hours	$ of assets	million BTUs	% of all manufacturing			
■ chemicals	8	1,039	22.4	9.0	5.5 ■	21.2	58.4 ■
paper	19	1,448	36.7	4.6	3.6	11.5	13.6
primary metal	24	1,581	45.9	4.3	4.0	14.0	12.5
refining & coal products	9	2,670	127.0	3.9	.8	31.2	3.7
transportation equipment	18	649	2.4	5.8	10.6	1.7	1.6
food products	17	665	7.6	8.7	8.4	4.8	1.4
electric machinery	20	695	2.2	10.0	10.7	1.1	1.4
■ non–electric machinery	20	677	2.0	9.5	10.7 ■	1.4	.4 ■
lumber & wood products	40	805	13.0	3.2	3.9	2.0	.2

Labor, capital, and energy requirements and pollution produced by manufacturing U.S. 1987/88

Industries	Inputs needed to generate $1,000 of value–added			GDP	employment	energy use	toxic release
	labor	capital	energy				
	hours	$ of assets	million BTUs	% of all manufacturing			
chemicals	8	1,039	22.4	9.0	5.5	21.2	58.4
paper	19	1,448	36.7	4.6	3.6	11.5	13.6
primary metal	24	1,581	45.9	4.3	4.0	14.0	12.5
refining & coal products	9	2,670	127.0	3.9	.8	31.2	3.7
transportation equipment	18	649	2.4	5.8	10.6	1.7	1.6
food products	17	665	7.6	8.7	8.4	4.8	1.4
electric machinery	20	695	2.2	10.0	10.7	1.1	1.4
non–electric machinery	20	677	2.0	9.5	10.7	1.4	.4
lumber & wood products	40	805	13.0	3.2	3.9	2.0	.2

Number of species in jeopardy compared to wilderness areas and protected land in countries of megadiversity compared to the United States

	species in jeopardy:			wilderness area (sq.miles)	protected land (sq.miles)
	mammals	birds	plants		
peru	29	65	353	141,544	21,304
ecuador	21	64	121	0	41,257
colombia	25	69	316	58,519	35,914
malaysia	23	35	na	10,981	4,487
china	30	83	841	813,807	84,738
madagascar	53	28	193	2,669	4,161
united states	21	43	2,476	170,108	379,698

Number of species in jeopardy compared to wilderness areas and protected land in countries of megadiversity compared to the United States

	species in jeopardy:			wilderness area (sq.miles)	protected land (sq.miles)
	mammals	birds	plants		
peru	29	65	353	141,544	21,304
ecuador	21	64	121	0	41,257
colombia	25	69	316	58,519	35,914
malaysia	23	35	na	10,981	4,487
china	30	83	841	813,807	84,738
madagascar	53	28	193	2,669	4,161
united states	21	43	2,476	170,108	379,698

4.
The density of the bars representing pollution is compared to the openness on the less polluting side. Color reinforces the comparison and the bar graph suggests a factory chimney.

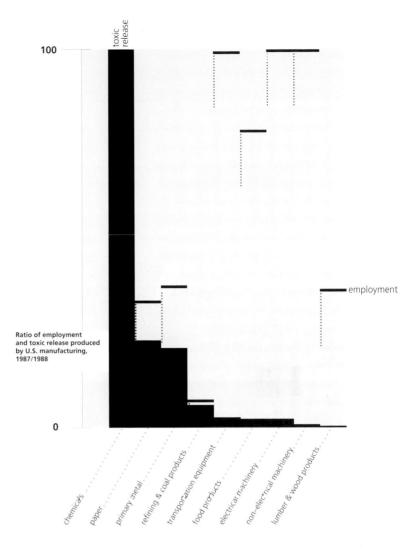

100

toxic release

employment

Ratio of employment and toxic release produced by U.S. manufacturing, 1987/1988

0

chemicals
paper
primary metal
refining & coal products
transportation equipment
food products
electrical machinery
non-electrical machinery
lumber & wood products

4.
Proportional display makes the issue of plant species in jeopardy a surprisingly immediate concern for U.S. residents. The protection of land is apparently not an effective deterrent to plant species destruction.

Encroachment on a leaf form and color corresponding to natural leaf deterioration make the point. Overly passive form or color would cancel the urgency of the message.

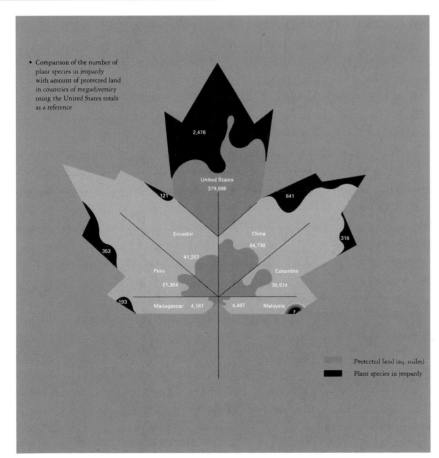

• Comparison of the number of plant species in jeopardy with amount of protected land in countries of megadiversity using the United States totals as a reference

2,476

United States
379,698

121

841

353

316

Ecuador
41,257

China
84,738

Peru
21,304

Colombia
35,914

193

Madagascar 4,161

4,487 Malaysia

7

Protected land (sq. miles)

Plant species in jeopardy

1.
Base
The base table as situated in the space to emphasize opening toward the right, supporting the lessening of restrictions.

2.
Extending the dotted line and box to the full dimension of the field emphasizes this feature.

3.
Tonal gradation works vertically to link countries in relation to the degrees of restriction while showing the progressive opening.

conditions under which abortions are allowed in selected
countries by region in relation to total number of abortion
and share of world population
1989

life endangerment	other maternal health reasons	social and socio-medical reasons	no mandated conditions	
Latin America:				
brazil costa rica	argentina	-		
chile	-	peru	-	
columbia	-	-	-	
mexico	-	-	-	
Europe:				
ireland	-	poland	italy	
-	-	united kingdom	france	
-	-	west germany	netherlands	
-	-	-	sweden	
-	-	-	czechoslovakia	
-	-	-	russia	
Asia:				
indonesia	-	india	china	
lebanon	-	-	-	
pakistan	-	-	-	
philippines	-	-	-	
bangladesh	-	-	-	
Africa/Mideast:				
nigeria	egypt	-		
sudan	ghana	-		
-	morocco	-	-	
-	zimbabwe	-		
-	israel	-		
North America:				
-	-	-	canada	
-	-	-	united states	
53	42	14	23	total number of countries
25%	12%	23%	40%	share of world population

conditions under which abortions are allowed in selected
countries by region in relation to total number of abortion
and share of world population
1989

life endangerment	other maternal health reasons	social and socio-medical reasons	no mandated conditions	
●●●●●●●●●●●●●●●●●●●●●●●●●●●●●●●●●●				
Latin America:				
brazil costa rica	argentina	-		
chile	-	peru	-	
columbia	-	-	-	
mexico	-	-	-	
Europe:				
ireland	-	poland	italy	
-	-	united kingdom	france	
-	-	west germany	netherlands	
-	-	-	sweden	
-	-	-	czechoslovakia	
-	-	-	russia	
Asia:				
indonesia	-	india	china	
lebanon	-	-	-	
pakistan	-	-	-	
philippines	-	-	-	
bangladesh	-	-	-	
Africa/Mideast:				
nigeria	egypt	-		
sudan	ghana	-		
-	morocco	-	-	
-	zimbabwe	-		
-	israel	-		
North America:				
-	-	-	canada	
-	-	-	united states	
53	42	14	23	total number of countries
25%	12%	23%	40%	share of world population

conditions under which abortions are allowed in selected
countries by region in relation to total number of abortion
and share of world population
1989

life endangerment	other maternal health reasons	social and socio-medical reasons	no mandated conditions	
Latin America:				
brazil costa rica	argentina	-		
chile	-	peru	-	
columbia	-	-	-	
mexico	-	-	-	
Europe:				
ireland	-	poland	italy	
-	-	united kingdom	france	
-	-	west germany	netherlands	
-	-	-	sweden	
-	-	-	czechoslovakia	
-	-	-	russia	
Asia:				
indonesia	-	india	china	
lebanon	-	-	-	
pakistan	-	-	-	
philippines	-	-	-	
bangladesh	-	-	-	
Africa/Mideast:				
nigeria	egypt	-		
sudan	ghana	-		
-	morocco	-	-	
-	zimbabwe	-		
-	israel	-		
North America:				
-	-	-	canada	
-	-	-	united states	
53	42	14	23	total number of countries
25%	12%	23%	40%	share of world population

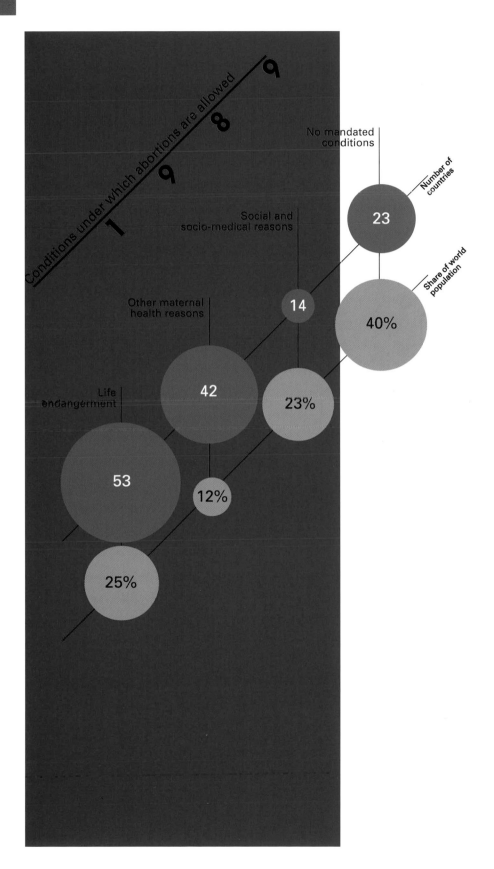

Conditions under which abortions are allowed

No mandated
conditions

Number of
countries

Share of world
population

23

Social and
socio-medical reasons

14

40%

Other maternal
health reasons

42

23%

Life
endangerment

53

12%

25%

Theme:
Recommended daily
vitamin and mineral
allowances for women.
An analogy to molecular
structure adds a
sense of the scientific
basis of the data.
Color reinforces the logic
of the groupings and
lends the image a game-
like quality.

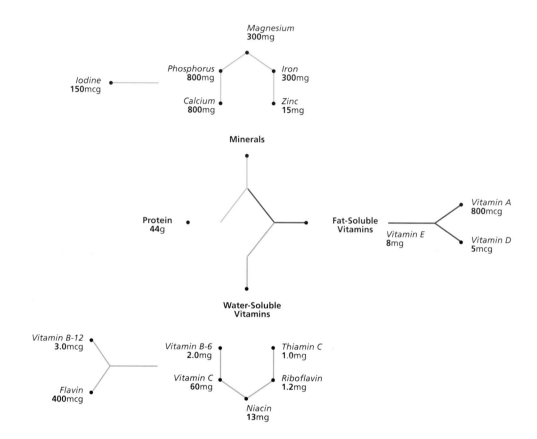

6.

the Built Environment

Architecture and architectural agglomerations form the large-scale context for graphic signs. In competitive contemporary urban culture the demand for signs that dominate the streetscape too often results in a cacophonic chaos that leads to rapid decay.

▼

In this chapter we look for ways to link the need for publicity with a consideration for the built environment to give the combined form integrity and uniqueness while solving the need for a dynamic street presence.

This brick-patterned street in Guarda, Switzerland, symbolizes the ideal of place without the interruptions of contemporary commercialism. The question is: Could signs placed in this street or any street attain the same measure of abstraction as the already dynamically placed apertures and other façade elements, for that is what determines the durability and rhythmic vitality of the street.

The street is the interface between commerce and citizens. It belongs to every- one

and no one.

The **Pulse** of the Street

The street is a rhythm of signs—visual street language. It is a rhythm of people in motion, of vehicles, signs, buildings, lighting, and sounds. Staccato-legato, loud-soft, formal-casual. Contrasting features make the hot and cold of the street. Massing redundant and self-stultifying features creates a tempest of visual illiteracy and hyperactivity.

These forces vary and combine in ways that make it impossible to choreograph them completely. The demand a total design imposes can be observed in the book *African Canvas* by Margaret Courtney-Clarke. In the villages of West Africa that she portrays, buildings and their ornamentation, every implement, every fabric and texture, every person and dress combine to make a harmonious yet highly differentiated environment. Cultures in which this has been achieved are rare, remote, and receding.

Choreography as a concept for managing

> *"The cities of the New World have one characteristic in common: that they pass from first youth to decrepitude with no intermediate stage....*
>
> *The older a European city is, the more highly we regard it; in America, every year brings with it an element of disgrace. For they (American cities) are not merely 'newly built'; they are built for renewal, and the sooner the better."*
>
> —Claude Lévi-Strauss

the movement of characters on stage can be applied metaphorically to any kind of design in which kinetic rhythm is an advantage. In fact, choreography of all kinds of design increases sensitivity to dynamic motion that both stimulates interest and aids memory—essential aspects of any communication. When rhythms are managed so that they also create an essential unity, they act as a positive discharge mechanism for aggressive and sexual energies. This is more than just an aesthetic achievement.

Is Main Street "All Right"?

In *Learning from Las Vegas,* Robert Venturi, Denise Scott Brown, and Steven Izenour defend the American commercial strip as almost all right. In thus repudiating purist design, they are asserting the value of a language based in common symbology and persuasive appeal. They are affirming the dramatic, improvisational character of the street that emerges when businesses constantly adjust their appeal to attract the market. They are affirming a narrative quality to which people easily relate instead of the alienating, elitist, abstract quality that is often held to characterize modernist design. And they are saying that the street choreographs itself, so to speak.

But what and where is "Main Street"? The Las Vegas strip—which they used as a site to study the iconography of the American street, or strip— epitomizes but hardly typifies the usual Main Street.

What *does* typify Main Street is the separation of architecture and messages of overt communication, the tendency to make messages independently assertive—to "pop," to separate from the environment—and to adjust language to a mass audience through the use of clichés.

The result is a relative chaos, a cacophony of messages and colors—a chaos of clamoring ego trips. But individuation that is mere ego trip will separate rather than integrate; the possibility of creating rhythmic counterpoint is forfeited. Assertive and yet integrating? The balance between these functions is what we seek if we wish to achieve both vitality and longevity in our work as designers.

It is a temptation to dismiss these accretions as beyond correction and to let them follow the laws of entropy. But there are accretions that have become richer with time. This is especially true in cultures where the layering of architecture and sign is less self-conscious, an outgrowth of a closely knitted society, where messages in the environment don't need to clamor for attention.

So the question is: What hope do we have of increasing the extent of wholeness in the built environment if the general movement is toward fragmentation? How do we avoid visual congestion that can't satisfy our psychological needs? In short, how do we avoid visual oppression in the built environment?

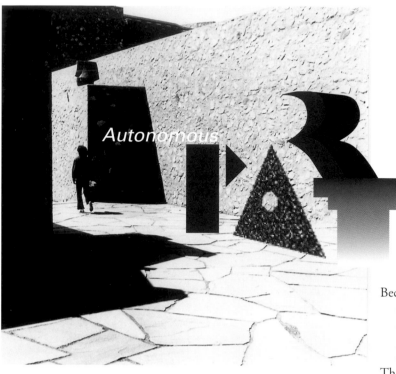

Autonomous **PARTS** *= Participation*

The person walking, each texture, each shadow, each plane, each letter superimposed—all maintain their autonomy as parts and by their extreme complementarity form a whole.

We begin by defining parts that are building blocks for an unpredictable whole. In a nonoppressive environment each part makes sense (contributes), has a place, and is through good proportioning allowed to express itself. A designer can provide the places for the parts, but the dynamic of placement is such that the viewer is actively involved in choosing the perceptual paths, in assembling the message and impression— and ultimately in completing the message. (The ever-changing and actual presence of people also significantly alters how we see the built environment at any given time.)

A further advantage of the autonomous parts concept is how it facilitates and accommodates change.

Because as humans we can be responsible only for parts of this environment, the question is how we can design these parts to enhance rather than degrade each other as change accrues over time.

This has much to do with our concept of signs and with our recognizing how signs are created and understood.

We must differentiate between

1. signs as any signifiers, intended or not, and

2. signs as combinations of letters and images as intentional, focused communication.

Signs as any signifiers include features, especially nonverbal ones, that affect how they are perceived. An architect can successfully design an entrance to function as a sign, but aspects of the entrance's color and texture and its use of natural elements will be interpreted differently by different people. Even the judgment as to whether a visual environment with many elements feels congested or

Rocks placed in a larger shape of gravel in a Japanese-style garden tell us how signs as "autonomous parts" could be integrated. Public sculptures like Claes Oldenburg's clothespin in Philadelphia and the sign pylon on the University of Pennsylvania campus show the possibility of integration while retaining separate identities, whether old or new.

> *"The incomplete building, like the semi-demolished one, holds the attention more than the complete form."*
> —Marshall McLuhan

lively will vary widely.

The nonverbal aspect of built design communication is more dependable in a closed culture where things are understood out of tradition. In a culture that brings people together randomly out of diverse cultures and orientations, the design of parts that serve their purpose and combine to build an uplifting experience is very demanding and often does not allow the time for reflection such projects require.

Signs as environmental graphics are typically self-explanatory. We should differentiate, however, between "signage"—thought of more as the tacked-on signboard—and "environmental graphics," which are designed to grow out of and integrate with their architectural sites. Effective environmental graphics complement the nonverbal aspects of buildings to create a symbiotic whole.

Positive Zoning

Zoning as a device of urban policy usually legislates restrictions to prevent gross intrusions onto a street's character. For example, projecting signs are prohibited between City Hall and Pine Street and many other streets in Center City Philadelphia. The result emphasizes building architecture and façade elements, including window displays. The reserved quality is appropriate here because many of the businesses that meet the street on South Broad Street are banks or other relatively "cool" enterprises. The addition of banners to this street creates a dynamic contrast that would be reduced if the banners were competing with other projecting signs.

A corporate design program is itself a kind of zoning—that is, a defining of how it should or should not be applied in varying circumstances. The mutually beneficial intersection of zoning that defines the identity of a specific enterprise and that which defines the street as a public place is difficult to achieve. Businesses and signmakers typically chafe under negative zoning restrictions. In their constant desire to do something different, they look for loopholes, ways to justify an exception. One approach to the problem of zoning is to shift a negative zoning code to a positive one that defines the character of the street and invites creativity within certain parameters, as in the example above.

The campus identity program for The University of the Arts, shown as a demonstration in this chapter, translates a restriction into a permission: projecting signs are avoided; instead, integral parallel-to-façade environmental graphics are used. Fidelity to the university's mission as an educational institution in the arts is expressed in the freedom with which the autonomous parts of a visual identity are site-specifically transformed.

A shop display in a street on the Greek island of Mykonos and the Taschist wall tapestry by Pierre Soulages for the news reading room of the library of the School for Economics in St. Gallen, Switzerland, show how implanted symbols can be harmoniously integrated with the architectural environment.

A student's proposal for linking four restaurants. A zoned approach creating vertical neon signs emphasizes the separate sign character of each building's architectural features.

Dentist,
plan and two views

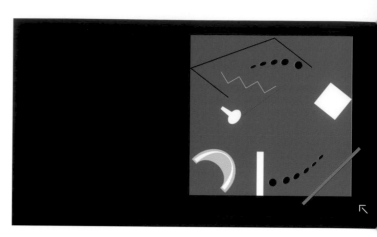

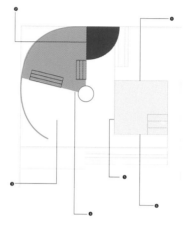

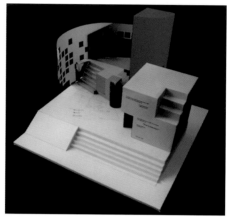

Architect,
plan with text location
pattern, left, and single
view

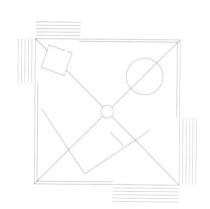

Philosopher,
plan and single view

Environmental Graphics:
Some Experiments

Practice in responding to three-dimen-
sional architectural environments can
come from creating structures that
integrate graphic messages and a three-
dimensional form.

In the projects shown here students
create definitions of professions in a walk-
through spatial environment they have
designed.

Each structure carries a range of
messages: the name and definition of
the profession, a salient feature of its
history, the voice of a prominent
practitioner of the field, education needed
for the field, and its tools, including a
recent technological development in the
field.

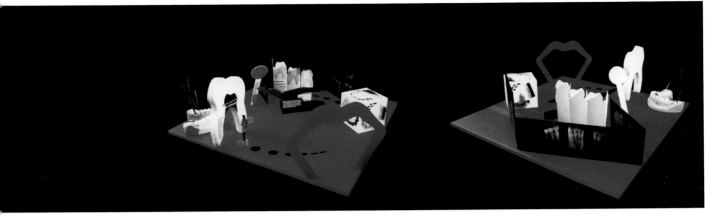

Rock musician,
plan and single view

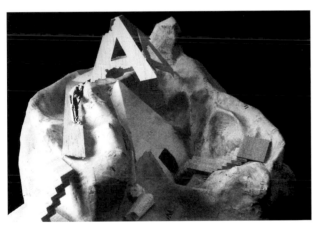

Archaeologist,
single view

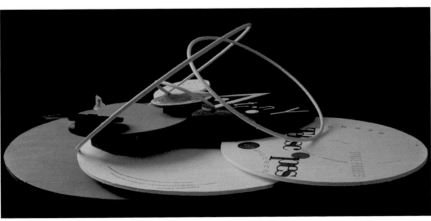

Astronomer,
single view

Project—
U/Arts Campus Identity Program:
Design a graphic identity and
adaptations in response to existing
built environments.

Goals:

Built environments with a history often feel more human and accessible than brand new ones. They are also more or less chaotic, having been built as accretions without special regard to other buildings on the street.

The campus of The University of the Arts presents an eclectic array of physically disconnected buildings—some more distinguished, some less — dispersed among other buildings in an urban environment of medium density.

Though the buildings were built in the time period 1830–1995, "neo" styles—Greek Revival and Gothic—extend the stylistic range, at least superficially. These buildings, except one, are ranged along a major six-lane street of Center City Philadelphia along the Avenue of the Arts. Buildings along the avenue are linked by unique sidewalk paving, street lighting, and plantings.

—to design a base image of letter forms drawn from primary architectural form, legible and having a clear rhythmic structure
—to adapt the base image to multiple sites of different architectural form, material, use, and street context
—to explore techniques for representing placement of signs two-dimensionally
—to create a rhythm of recurrence and reinforcement of the base theme in the street while adding to the street's dynamic quality
—to achieve a reciprocal relation between each building's character and use and the applied graphic, each enhancing the other
—to replace verbal signs with visual signs or cues that declutter
—to observe functional parameters for legibility

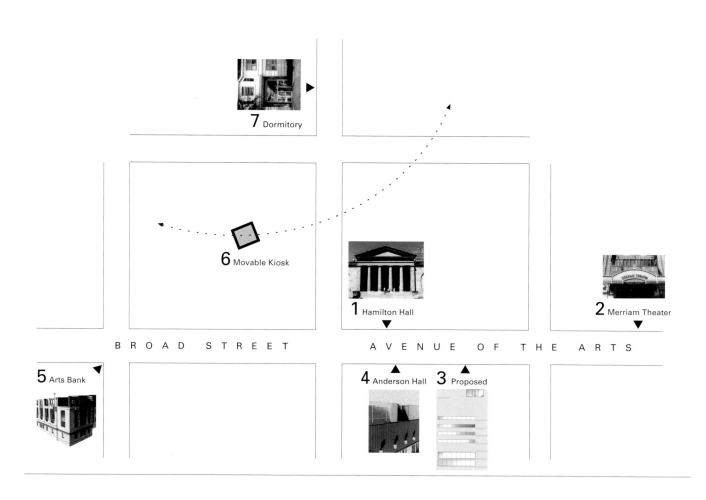

7 Dormitory

6 Movable Kiosk

1 Hamilton Hall

2 Merriam Theater

B R O A D   S T R E E T

A V E N U E   O F   T H E   A R T S

5 Arts Bank

4 Anderson Hall   3 Proposed

The parts echo, mimic, or allude to forms expressed in the elevation view of the building.

Relative importance of factors influencing design

Of the four forces affecting the design of the logo, the more solid, durable, and traditional ones are most determining. The sliding arrows indicate the relative importance of each factor. (The closer the arrowhead to the center, the stronger the influence.) For the applications on the following pages, the balance of influences changes as shown by the small-scale diagram of the four forces.

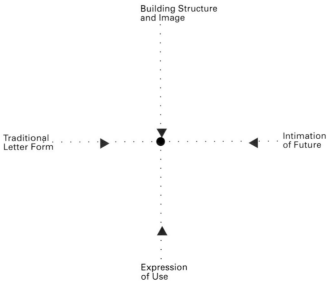

Building Structure
and Image

Traditional
Letter Form

Intimation
of Future

Expression
of Use

Testing the rhythmics and adaptability of the logotype before application

Testing depth of rhythmic contrast:

 punctuation/letter

 dot, line, mass

 geometric/free form

symmetric/asymmetric

wide letter/narrow letter

small/large

initial/word

Testing survival of form when distorted

Testing survival of form when compounded

Testing survival of form when interrupted

Testing survival of form in noisy environment

Testing survival of form when contaminated

Testing survival of form when compacted

Testing clarity of
autonomous parts under
conditions of changed
dimensionality,
lighting, material, view-
point, and configuration

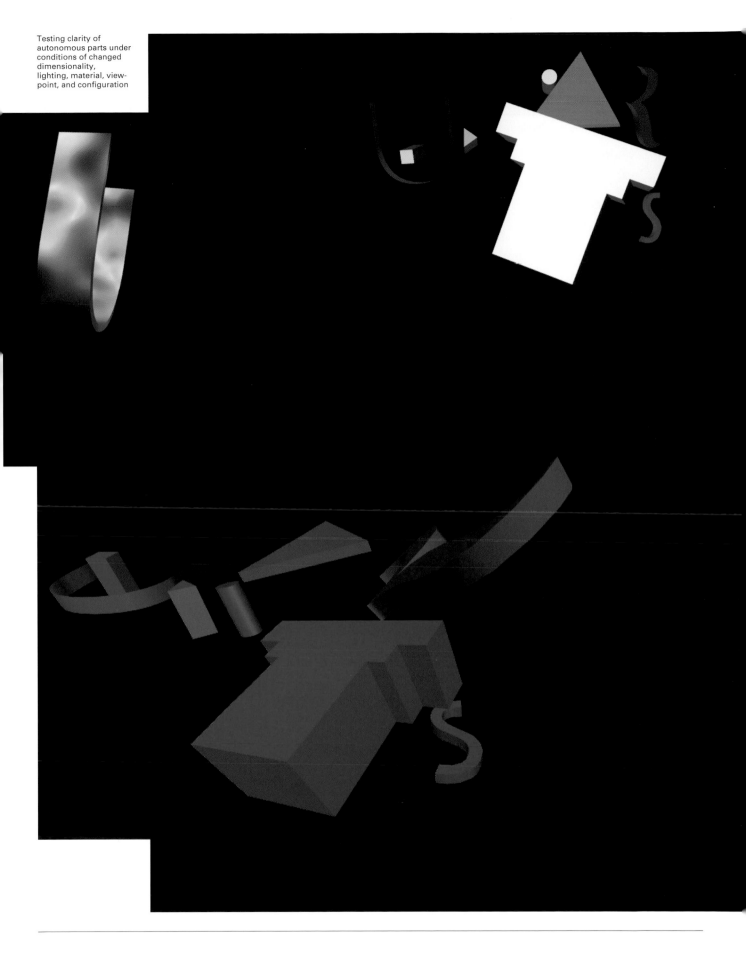

The Greek Revival façade was designed by John Haviland for the Pennsylvania Institution for the Deaf and Dumb in 1824. The Greek temple style has been appropriated by enterprises of all kinds, including banks—and, in Philadelphia, the waterworks! It projects alternately an imposing, intimidating quality and a familiar, traditional accessibility.
In the original design, Haviland incorporated manual sign language as a decorative façade element. These elements were removed as the building's use changed. It is now the central administrative and meeting locale of the university.

The setback from the street presents various possibilities for solving the graphic identity question, including
1. freestanding elements
2. elements tightly integrated with façade
3. suspended elements in relation to the columnar structure
4. combinations.
The building itself functions as sign. It is key for drawing out the basic U/Arts identity elements. An approach that expresses this source relationship, with tightly integrated elements, might be considered ideal and has been adopted for the application chosen. Warm-

toned stone unifies the columns and other elements in the existing façade. This color is retained in the molded logotype elements, lending a quiet dignity to the uncompromisingly modern letter forms.

As is often the case with older buildings, additions have created hybrid structures. In the case of the Haviland building, a large-scale addition designed by Frank Furness in 1875 has added an aspect in strong contrast to the Greek Revival façade. A detail is shown. Especially characteristic are the red brick material and the use of the brick module to create stepped decorative patterns. In drawing on the essential geometry of the Greek source, however, a connection is also made to the Furness architecture.

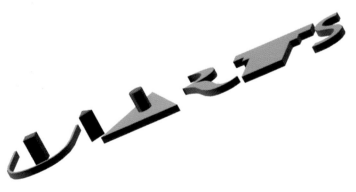

Night view

To mediate more obviously between the Haviland and Furness building features, the small elements can be accented in red. In one instance the stone-colored base is preserved; in the second, a satin metallic construction introduces a material equally in contrast to stone and brick.

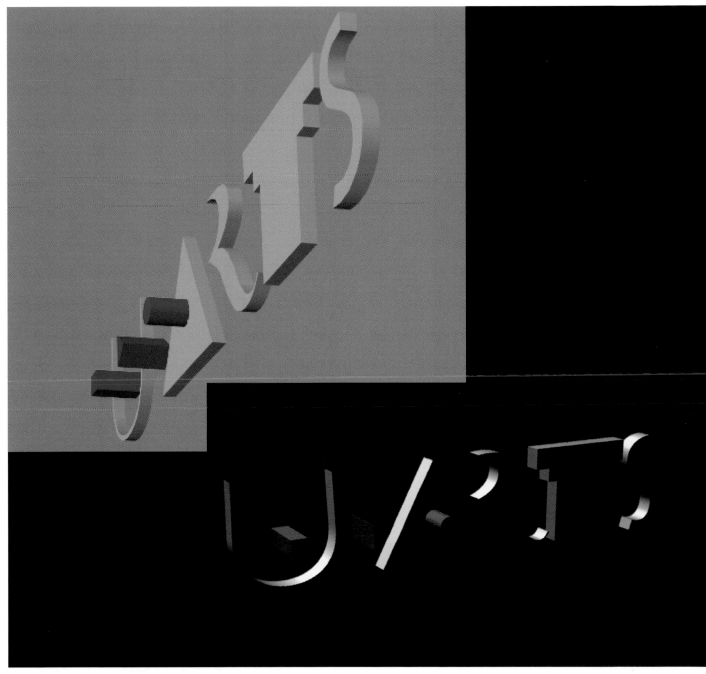

Characteristic detail of Furness Dormitory, connected to Hamilton Hall but not visible from Broad Street— geometry built from brick modules.

177

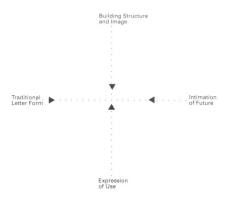

Building Structure
and Image

Traditional ▶ .... ▼ .... ◀ Intimation
Letter Form   ▲   of Future

Expression
of Use

This building was built in 1918 with a patterned red brick and muted pink stone façade. A marquee was redesigned and added in 1988. Although the theater is part of the university campus and houses a large segment of the College of Performing Arts space, the building's street presence is as a theater for the general public. Its identity as a commercial theater—specifically as the Merriam Theater—is primary. In addition, publicity for specific theater events may subsume the building's identity.

Banners are a way to introduce the U/Arts identity in color and form derived from the building without confusing the already complex façade. The modular quality of a banner system allows for event-oriented banners to replace the U/Arts banner when this is desirable, or for the U/Arts banner to be used in multiple when no events are occurring in the theater.

The graphic treatment of the banner introduces playful elements suggesting a multiplanar stage, mutable for variation over time.

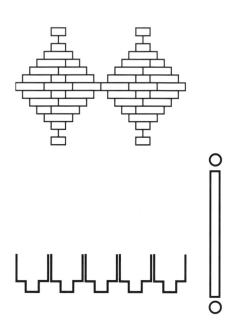

A frayed version of the image tests its coherency under environmental duress while suggesting another expressive dimension of this treatment.

The notched edge, as an additional banner feature, mimics the edge of the marquee.

3
Proposed New Media Building

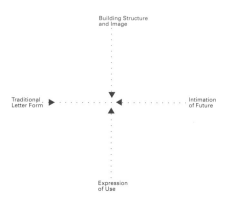

Building Structure
and Image

Traditional
Letter Form

Intimation
of Future

Expression
of Use

The building is planned to house performing
arts studios and new media laboratories.
The proposed façade treatment is the product of
the simultaneous design of building and
graphics. The unique image presented by the
combination of building and graphics gives a
sense of newly emerging forms while avoiding
trendy, easily dated shapes.

The shift in lighting changes what are perceived
as shadow forms by day to illuminated
elements at night. The graphics combine with
the unpredictable interior illumination at
night to project a sense of stage and screen.
By day the building and graphic colors combine
as a soft and optimistic composite.

As noted in the diagram, this version most
strongly converges building form, expression of
use, and intimations of the future.

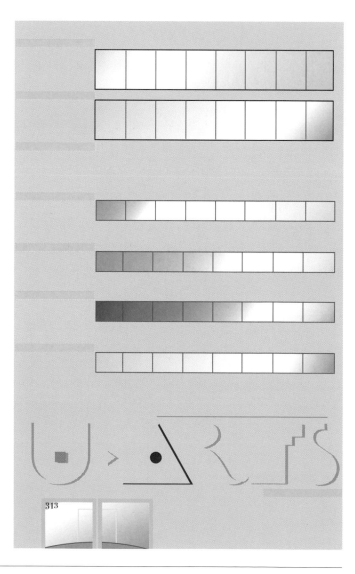

The plan view shows the
interrelation of elements
in the façade. The
convex window line is in
rhythmic relation to
the extent of protrusion of
graphic elements.

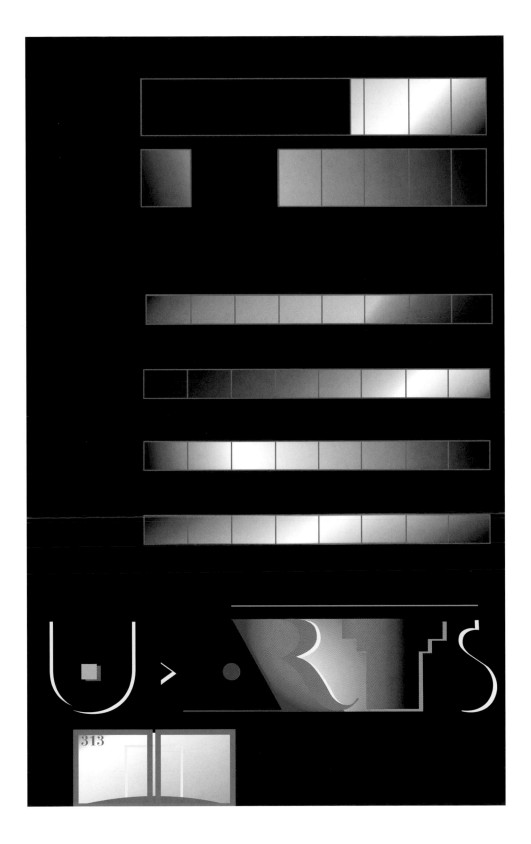

4.1
Anderson Hall

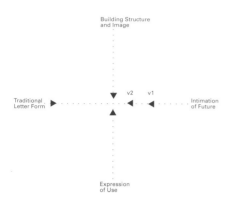

Building Structure
and Image

Traditional
Letter Form ▶ · · · · · · · · ▼ v2 ◀ ◀ v1 ◀ · · · · · Intimation
of Future
▲

Expression
of Use

Anderson Hall was built in 1921 as a parking garage and was later adapted to diverse industrial uses. It was renovated in 1985 as the main studio space for the College of Art and Design. The anonymous façade of stone and ordinary fenestration was modified by the opening of show windows for the ground-level gallery and the addition of a decorative bronze-colored metal fascia section extending to the second story.

The window nearest the entrance is the location for changing exhibition advertisements. These windows vary substantially in character and dynamic expression. Any approach to the U/Arts identity, besides drawing from the color, proportion, and entrance quality of the building, should acknowledge and allow the incorporation of the new and changing elements that stem from the exhibition program.

The version on the left retains the base form of the logo while responding to the vertical striation of the surface.
The second version compacts the logo in larger scale for stronger expression against the neutral industrial façade.

4.2
Anderson Hall Wall Graphic

The windowless side of Anderson Hall from the seventh to the tenth floor has functioned as a painted, billboard scale advertisement in the past. The space above the church next to it provides good visibility to this area. As part of the U/Arts identity program, the space offers an opportunity for a more extravagant interpretation. Paint is used to create an economical large-scale, trompe l'oeil image. Three variations are shown.

Elements are used and placed to provide a degree of recursivity to shapes of the neo-Gothic church architecture. The "U" used elsewhere is replaced by a more massive form deriving from the church tower structure. This gives the whole image a stronger impact.

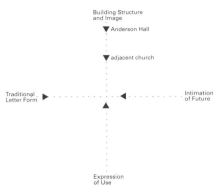

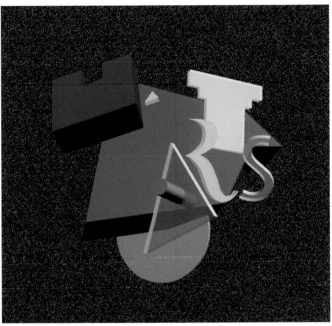

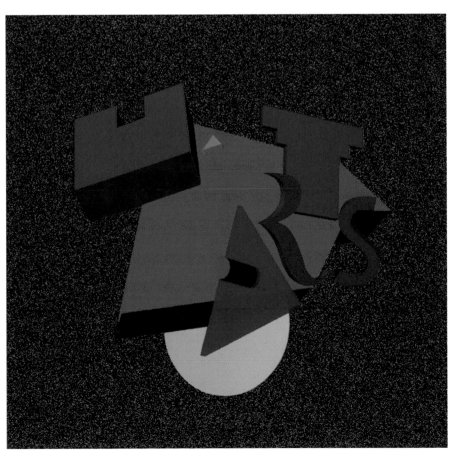

5.1
Arts Bank Theater Corner Column

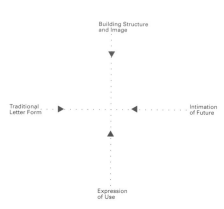

Building Structure
and Image

▼

Traditional · · · ▶ · · · · · · · · · ◀ · · · Intimation
Letter Form   of Future

▲

Expression
of Use

5.2
▼

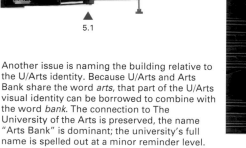

▲
5.1

The building was originally a commercial bank
built in massive Art Deco style after World War I
and replicated in Philadelphia many times over.
Its previous life and purpose is retained in the
external architecture and in the name, giving it
a unique identity. As a theater, its interior has
undergone dramatic renovation, creating a deep
space for experimental productions with a
contemporary foyer and service areas.

In its new guise the Arts Bank is again a place of
transactions, this time of a human kind—
between and among players, between players
and audience. These "transactions" are dynamic, colorful, entertaining, exciting, and stimulating; the idea of the bank is infused with new
meaning.

Graphic reidentification corresponds in extravagance to the building's new purpose and
derives from its interior form and usage. Its
corner location with good visibility on the
Avenue of the Arts expands the possibility for
dramatic graphics. Such an approach stands in
sharp contrast to the solid exterior, where only
the Art Deco subtleties connect expressively to
the new purpose. More formal connection can
also be made to the larger elements—aperture
shape and size, implied column dimensions,
etc.
The options for applying a dynamic graphic
identity include:
1.
wrapping elements around the corner at a
normal marquee height in the band just above
the ground-floor windows
2.
concentrating elements at the entrance on the
corner
3.
placing elements into the building surface
throughout its height
4.
mounting elements on the roof
5.
combinations of these.

Options 2, the corner column, and 4, the roof
mount, are the focus of this application. Within
each option the additional possibilities for
relating letter and form are described in the
matrix on pages 190–191. The options vary in
cost according to materials, degree of anima-
tion, and lighting change. In each case lighting
plays a key role in relation to competing street
and commercial lighting.

Another issue is naming the building relative to
the U/Arts identity. Because U/Arts and Arts
Bank share the word *arts*, that part of the U/Arts
visual identity can be borrowed to combine with
the word *bank*. The connection to The
University of the Arts is preserved, the name
"Arts Bank" is dominant; the university's full
name is spelled out at a minor reminder level.

Enlarging the corner
support column
draws attention to the
entrance using existing
support.

5.2
Arts Bank Roof Mount

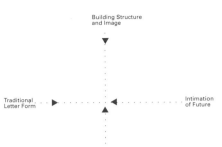

Building Structure
and Image
▼

Traditional . . . ▶ · · · · · ◀ Intimation
Letter Form ▲ of Future

Expression
of Use

The letter "U" is deleted
from the vocabulary since
it is not part of the Arts
Bank name. The theater
retains a visual connection
to the university while
identifying it as a venue
serving the larger
community.

A pole concept stacks the
elements shish-kebab-like
on a single support
that contains a mechanism
for controlled rotation
speed. Varying speeds
and arcs of rotation permit
control of the many
combinations.

More examples of
configurations that result
from programming
rotating elements in
relation to stationary ones
are shown on the next
page.

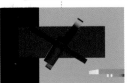

Plan view of the pole
structure

6
Pine Street Dormitory

Building Structure
and Image

Traditional
Letter Form

Intimation
of Future

Expression
of Use

The Pine Street Dormitory is a multistory red brick building built as a residence for itinerant salesmen in 1914. The first two stories are clad in stone veneer and the entrance is framed in dark green marble. Compared with the Avenue of the Arts a block away, Pine Street is quieter, darker, and largely residential.

Preserving a quiet tone to the graphic identification seems appropriate for defining a home for students, a place of privacy in which personal identity can be asserted within personal spaces. An economical and unobtrusive solution to preserve the transparency of the entrance and foyer and its existing lighting is appropriate for a building that contrasts in its introspection with the other buildings, all of which are extroverted to varying degrees.

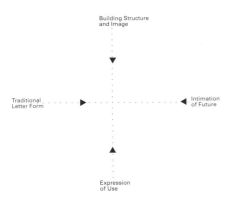

7
Promotional Kiosk

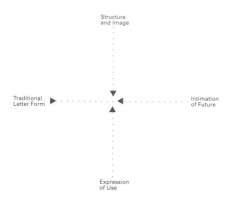

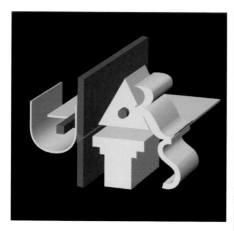

Graphic form that is clear in its fundamental geometry lends itself, as has been shown, to three-dimensional extension. Taken to an extreme, it becomes a kind of building in its own right. Adjustments bring the elements into proximity for the sake of connectedness. An added larger element provides the massive foil for the more fragile linear letters.

The purpose of a mobile kiosk is to charge larger interior display spaces with a three-dimensional presence.

Two ways of assembling the elements. The one shown below is primarily decorative.

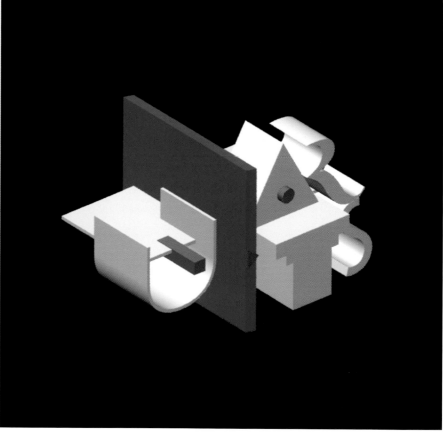

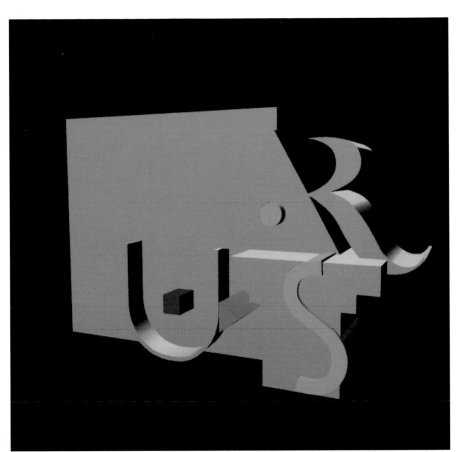

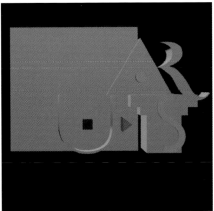

A more massive treatment allows for enclosure of promotional materials and a surface for display. The structure could be perforated with additional apertures for computer terminal display.

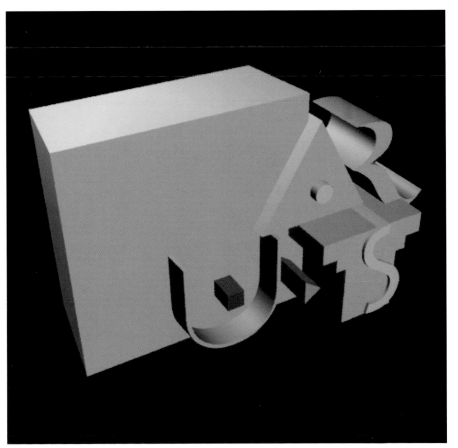

Physical Factors			1	2	3	3
Material		cloth		●		
		glass				
		metal				
		plastic				
		composite			●	●
		stone	●			
Material Qualities		matte ● / ○ glossy	●	●	●	○
		smooth ● / ○ rough	●	●	●	○
		rigid ● / ○ flexible	●	○	●	●
		stationary ● / ○ moving	●	○	●	●
		opaque ● / ○ transparent	●	●	●	○
		flat ● / ○ three-dimensional	●	●	●/○	●/○
Method of Production		etched				
		painted				
		cut out	●			
		molded			●	
		screen printed		●		
		light tubing				
		holographic				●
Color		single red				
		mixed warm/cool reds				
		red + complements		●		
		red + cools				
		neutrals	●		●	●
Mounting		free-standing				
		removable				
		surface mounted	●	●		
		surface integral			●	●
		projecting				
		suspended		●		
Shape		geometric	●	●	●	●
		free-form	●	●	●	●
Lighting		ambient	●	●		
		reflected direct	●	●		
		internal				
		back				●
		light is image				●
Relation to Building		integral/blend			●	
		integral/contrast	●			●
		separate		●		
Contextual Factors			1	2	3	3
Function		inform	●			
		identify	●	●	●	●
		orient	●	●		
		interpret		●	●	●
		persuade		●	●	●
		entertain		●	●	●
		embellish	●	●	●	●
Duration		short, event-related		●		
		one year				
		several years				
		long term	●		●	●
Viewing Distance		close ±8 ft.				
		middle ±30 ft.	●		●	●
		far 100 ft. +	●	●	●	●
Vertical Placement		ground level				
		eye-level				
		door height				
		fascia height	●		●	●
		upper-story level		●		
		top				
Legibility		conventional	●		●	
		eccentric		●		●

Recapitulation of physical and contextual factors, binary representation

For a detailed description, read vertically down to each application shown at right.

By reading horizontally within each group of factors, one can trace the rhythm of changes from one application to the next.

See page 192 for a summary statement regarding the sign program.

1 ▼ 2 ▼ 3 ▼ ▼

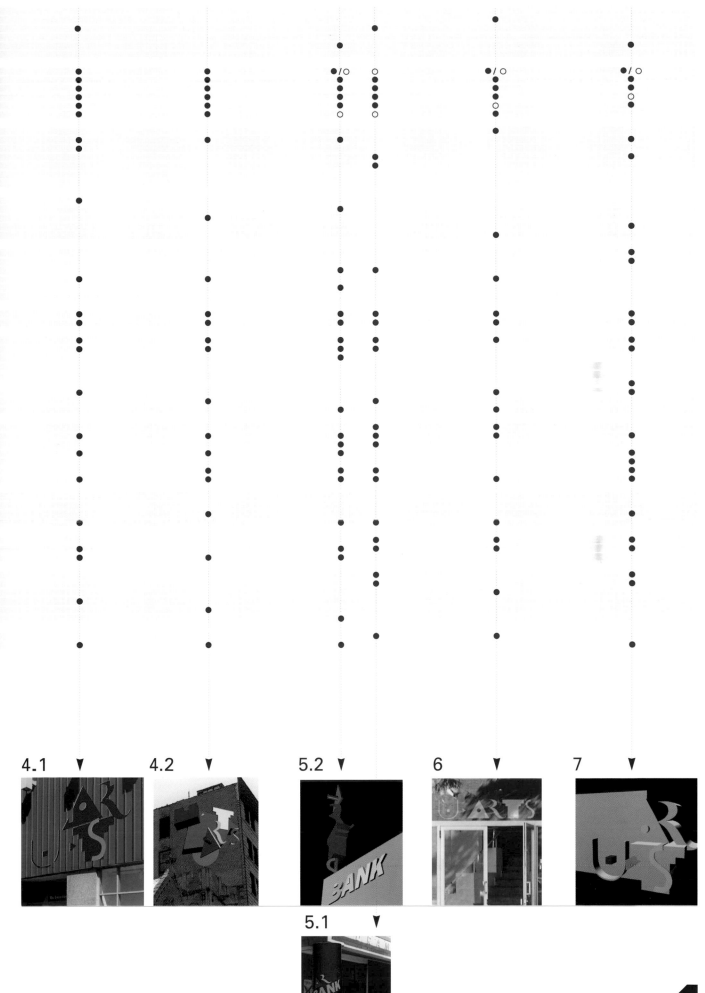

4.1   ▼

4.2   ▼

5.2 ▼

6   ▼

7   ▼

5.1   ▼

Summary

The matrix overleaf provides additional detail regarding physical and contextual factors for each type of sign. Placing each sign's qualities into the matrix allows these qualities to be compared with the larger range of possibilities at the same time that comparisons with other signs in the family are made. Revisions in design can thus be put in relation to other related decisions.

Materials are listed in a general way in the matrix.

A completely different and valid response to the range of architectural styles could have been a consistent treatment, perhaps like the Haviland-Strickland and Pine Street Dormitory designs. The approach chosen brings color to an otherwise monochromatic street. The strip at the bottom of the matrix summarizes the program.

The project was undertaken as an independent study without economic or other constraints; rather, the goal was to examine possibilities of image variation and continuity in relation to given architectural styles.

Footnote to chapter 6:

In comparison with architectural applications where the image elements are almost always of necessity fabricated from specific materials, print applications allow the free play of fantasy with elements without regard for gravity or physical durability.

Drawing from . . .

Vernacular Expression

"Low design"—the vernacular—tantalizes by its accessibility. But the trained designer faces a dilemma here: on one hand, to assess and understand peculiar strength of the vernacular; on the other, to realize how evasive these qualities can be in problem-solving.

In this chapter we examine examples of messages that defy the stylistic purity of "high" design for their contribution to conscious and refined design. Interspersed are student projects exploring possibilities for a book cover design that contrasts "raw" and "cooked" as analogies to common and refined.

*Vernacular:
expression without self-conscious
deliberation;
intuitive and experience-based,
whether grass-roots
or sophisticated.*

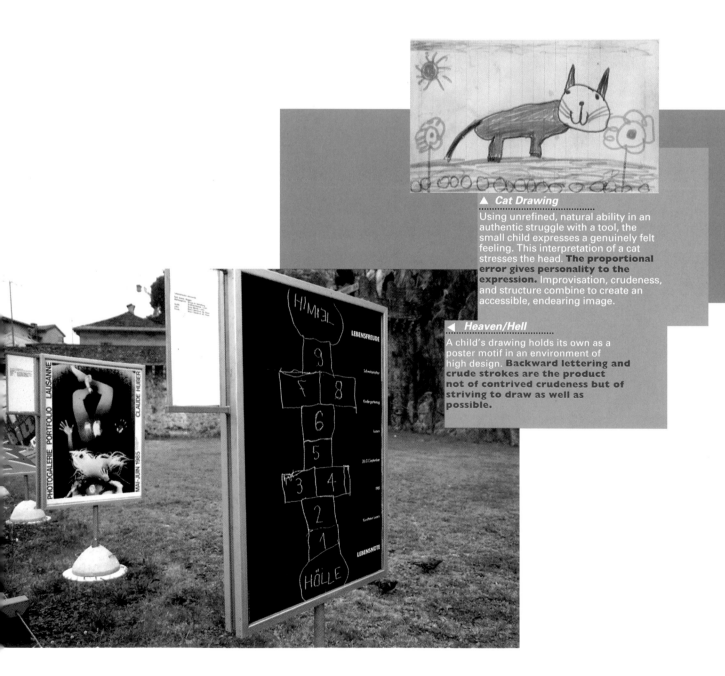

▲ **Cat Drawing**

Using unrefined, natural ability in an
authentic struggle with a tool, the
small child expresses a genuinely felt
feeling. This interpretation of a cat
stresses the head. **The proportional
error gives personality to the
expression.** Improvisation, crudeness,
and structure combine to create an
accessible, endearing image.

◄ **Heaven/Hell**

A child's drawing holds its own as a
poster motif in an environment of
high design. **Backward lettering and
crude strokes are the product
not of contrived crudeness but of
striving to draw as well as
possible.**

The human qualities of the vernacular often associated with "low design"—

crudeness, audacity, extravagance, directness, spareness, humor, childlikeness, spontaneity, earthiness—

offset the pretentiousness and affectation of over-refinement.

— AND TASTE

"Genius is childhood recaptured."
—CHARLES BAUDELAIRE

Vernacular forms of expression—whether spoken or written or visual—are those unrefined utterances formulated spontaneously when the unself-conscious mind responds in nimble terms to everyday circumstances. Vernacular expression is motivated by directness and convenience; it has a certain efficiency about it. We might, it follows, count these among vernacular forms: clichés, idioms, jargon, slang, shop talk, popularized technical terms, and vulgarizations.

Vernacular expression can be either mundane and routine or a manifestation of a kind of genius, the kind Baudelaire probably had in mind: that which is analogous to a child's raw inventive expression. This "genius" has to do with finding something for the first time, of being surrounded by the delight and surprise of discovery.

Such expressions, prevalent in the child's world, are less frequent in the more programmed world of adults. As adults we often admire the expressions of children for their freshness. In the same way we are especially receptive to words and idioms in other cultures or contexts that remind us of that childlike freshness.

Of course, an expression may be seen as unique simply because it is being perceived out of context. Most of the examples of the vernacular included in this chapter were found on my travels. Whether the power many of these signs exude is acknowledged by the indigenous people in any of these places is a question a stranger can't really determine. For the natives of any given culture or subculture, regardless of its level of sophistication, the indigenous language will seem natural and useful; its users may be conscious of its power in a completely different way from the outsider who is experiencing it for the first time. And yet, they may think it just ordinary, perhaps embarrassingly common. In this case the (naive) traveler, attuned to seeking the unfamiliar, finds that these expressions have a transcending value or dynamic quality or a refreshing humanness. The aspect of context is discussed later in this chapter.

Everyone uses vernacular speech, expressing thoughts spontaneously. When adults in our culture use visual language, they often choose a stiff and stilted manner that—if it were speech—would seem inhibited and unnatural. We attempt somehow to emulate a sophisticated visual style we admire and allow this to define our capabilities. Yet we wouldn't think of talking in the same mannered way! Only in young children does there typically seem to be a match between the vernacular of speech and of visual expression. (Ten-year-old boys drawing spaceships and gruesome creatures may still be in sync with their excited verbal outbursts.) We develop and educate our sense of taste. Encouraged by conventional understanding to rein in tendencies that might be considered anarchic and primitive, we separate ourselves from the natural and ordinary, confusing and subverting the natural development of visual and verbal expression.

Adolescents and adults alike may admire slick visual technique even when the visual image lacks essential visual quality—including rhythm, formal relationship, expression of the carrier medium, and creative insight. An admiration for technical wizardry increases when the wizardry, especially that of the digital electronic revolution, enables effects of stagecraft beyond our immediate grasp. A child's inventive imagining is supplanted by the magic of fawning imaging. The loss is substantial. At the least, it distances most people from a capacity for visual self-expression, rendering their creativity irrelevant.

The preservation of naturalness and spontaneity is an ideal of "high" design. This goal is in conflict with the urge to refine an image. The refined image can easily turn out stiff, mannered, slick, deceptive, or empty.

Taste ideally adds quality to raw impulses, preserving their essential power. When taken to an extreme, however, cultivated taste easily becomes artificial and stilted, lacking presence, power, and meaning.

The philosopher Immanuel Kant thought that in the pursuit of taste, the side of taste (the refined) should be favored:

"Taste, like judgment in general, is the discipline (or corrective) of genius. It severely clips its wings, and makes it orderly or polished; but at the same time it gives it guidance, directing and controlling its flight."

▲ *Simple Food*

Haute cuisine benefits from the infusion of the raw and the rural for both health and freshness.

Bursts of genius out of the vernacular give us a freshness that is often missing in highly refined design or that is destroyed in the development of taste.

Graphic design is the design of communication. The practice of design ultimately involves judgment, discipline, and discernment. The satisfactory reconciliation of raw impulse and controlling taste is an elusive goal for work that has a short life and must often be accomplished quickly. It is arduous and rewarding.

Using predetermined expressions—especially appropriating the refined idioms of the past—is the easy way out.

conductivity v. semiotic pollution

If vernacular expression is both authentic and accessible, then it has a special appeal for communication: ease of connection or conductivity. This is what the designer normally wants.

Design succeeds when it prevents complexity from overtaking intelligibility to users. Often the vernacular of a subculture, for example, a technological subculture of a highly specialized field, is too complex or too abbreviated to reach a general audience. Although the vernaculars of subcultures can thus be counterproductive and exclusionary, the use of everyday language can also make complex material accessible to a broader audience. It removes the veil imposed by brandishing complexity or in-group arrogance.

Seen another way, this is an ecological issue:

"Three important evolutionary tendencies are currently at work: (1) the increasing speed of the processes of production and consumption that result in built-in obsolescence and the throw-away nature of many products; (2) the increased sophistication of services that lead to the appearance of "mutable products," which entail diverse and complex services; and (3) the multiplication of linguistic codes in the definition of form that leads to a formal specification of products in relation to precise and limited user groups. . . .

*In evolving along this path, however, the system of artifacts collides with limitations—scarcity of resources, physical pollu-*tion and waste generation, sensorial pollution, **and semiotic pollution. . . . the (designed) object can increase its functions but not beyond the point of intelligibility."**

By using inflection in speech we emphasize, dramatize, and articulate thought. Inflected typography makes spoken language visible, increasing accessibility.

We must ask ourselves, though: Is imagined inflection, which is necessary when we read a book of monotonous visual character (text in the same font, all printed the same size—not at all how we speak), superior in any way to visually supported inflection? A significant part of the participatory act of reading is the fact that something is left for the reader's imagination. It might follow, then, that the interpretation of texts into visual equivalents could negate the power of the text more than it would support it. Is added visual inflection merely a concession to an age of shortened attention spans and increased fragmentation? Does inflection really assist the transfer of meaning or does the experience of the text perhaps diminish when reading becomes visually pleasurable?

A balance must be sought: the addition of "color" to a text can enhance or detract from its meaning. To excite to superficial acceptance or superficial reading is usually an insufficient goal. Seducing the reader into reading something that turns out to be trivial and not worth the reader's time will usually backfire.

A Ford Lately?

Advertising slogans capitalize on cliché expressions derived from vernacular speech. Frequent exposure to slogans produces a high degree of recognition by the general public. A slogan for the Ford Motor Company is interpreted with inflection. Each variation on the slogan has characteristics of emphasis that derive from a particular way of speaking the words. These characteristics combine with other elements of visual language to create a richer visual expression of the slogan. **Design can reinforce predictable inflection or alter it to create a specific emphasis**.

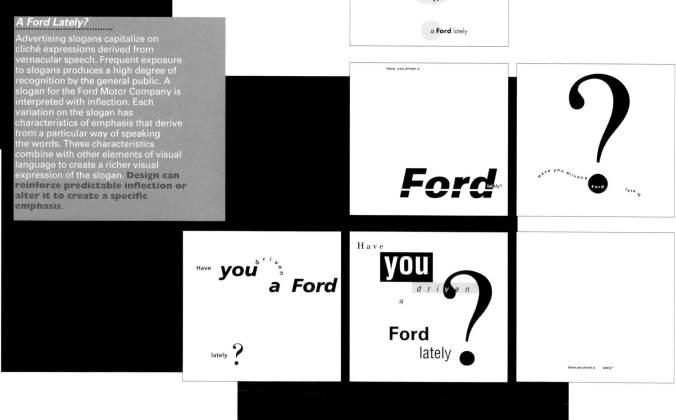

Every in-group, regardless of its level of sophistication, develops its own "dialects," and graphic design is no exception.

The vernaculars of graphic design include—besides a way of talking about visual language and information theory—fonts, clip art, and software manipulation options. They are delivered as neutral readymades (classic typefaces), as stylistic readymades (rogue typefaces and most clip art), and as readymade options for direct appropriation or further manipulation. A borrowed image is by definition not tailored to your specific message. **The challenge is to transcend the clichéd application of any of these readymades.**

Type Styles

Typefaces are means to create forms authentic to the reproduction processes, **but type styles of the past, which may have corresponded with the language of the past, are not necessarily in keeping with contemporary spoken language.**

(e.g., wedding invitation = Old English Text)

Recipes for the application of type style freeze the vernacular. By comparison, true emotional impact throws the formulaic to the side. Regarding the phenomenal skill of the Russian filmmaker Sergei Eisenstein, David Mayer writes that **"his ability obeyed no editing rules or experience espoused by others, anywhere.** It lay in his intuitive, assured frame-by-frame reassembly of filmed 'shots' to produce the emotional impact he had visualized for each scene, many improvised, during the shooting."

Clip Art

Clip art is an increasingly sophisticated and therefore dangerous phenomenon. The danger lies not in the use of readymade images per se but in the false sense of creativity they induce. **Clip art could be called the graphic equivalent to Musak, from which all "offensive or stimulating elements have been removed,"** as Ann Gould describes it.

Today the danger may be a glut of (fake) stimuli out of proportion to the message.

Software Menus

Planting a garden is a proportioning act. The skill to turn seeds with varying blooming times and color and foliage into a cohesive visual idea is extremely demanding. Anyone can get *something* to grow, but few can create a garden we would all identify as having a special quality. **Planted, seeds make a more or less predictable kind of flower, but the flower aggregate in the garden may be a mere chaos of color rather than a color idea.** (This could result in a certain accidental effect more effective by chance than any planned one might be.) Software options for manipulating type and image are an example of what happens when the vernacular of a technological subculture (graphic design and printing) proliferates. Like a seedrack, **the plethora of software options suggests and stimulates: they can be lifted to a level beyond the mundane, but to control each function and arrive at the right result usually requires extensive experimentation.** "Raw," here, is the product of options in two different programs.

▼

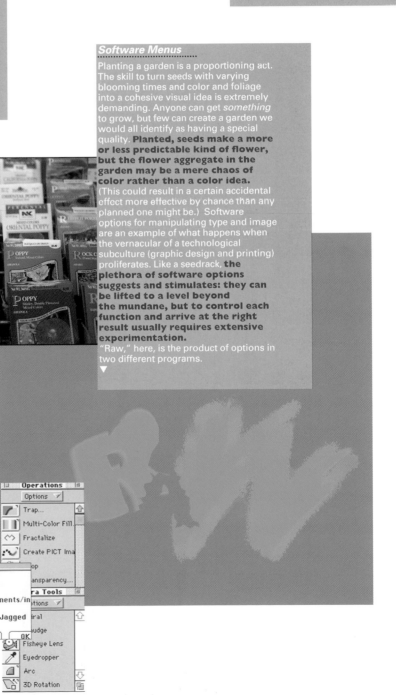

"Hi!, low, and in between"

In this interpretation, "low" design influences the pun on "high" and produces an intentionally congenial image. Rather than resolve the tension between high and low design by a true process of cross-fertilization, as this example does, a token approach is often taken. A vernacular element is inserted merely as a "warmer," something cute. **Lurking behind the tension of high and low is the question of "lifting," as in theft, and lifting as refinement, in which values of a vernacular rather than its specific forms are borrowed with integrity.**

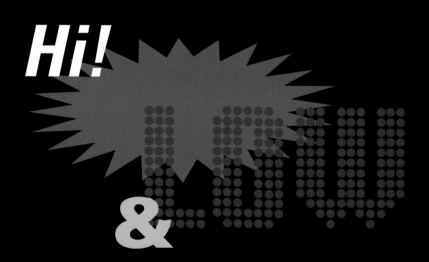

Yellow Page Ads

Yellow Pages rarely go beyond the most mundane packing in of information, severely cluttered and relying heavily on vernacular and stereotyped expression. Here five advertisements each extract one idea from the original advertisement shown above. **They retain or introduce a vernacular visual component, but the application of high design greatly increases the ad's legibility and impact through scale change and spatial dynamics.** The result is a lifting to something in between. From being attuned to the rhythm of spoken language, we can learn the "timing" of words in type on the page. Imagine the original Yellow Page ad as speech—something akin to ranting.

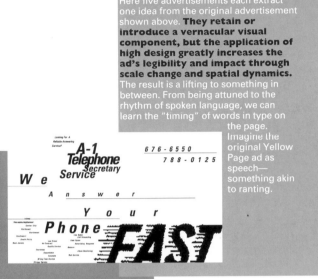

Thought is a non- linear

process.

"Cognitive research, has demonstrated that thought is a relative process made of responses newly generated moment by moment, using every part of the body, in which even memory is reconstituted, virtually from scratch, each time it is activated. The dissolution of time and space, discontinuity, and non-linearity have been shown to be the nature of the mind, not traces of barbarism."
—*Frances Butler*

Noam Chomsky maintains that what a person says is hardly a reliable guide to what a person actually knows, often unconsciously. This suggests that in impromptu speech or impromptu image-making, something is revealed that takes from both the conscious and subconscious mind. In the revelation of the moment, there is the possibility of natural expressions that are really much more functional than those prescribed by formal grammar. Equally, there is the possibility of messages veiled by the noise of imperfection. Because it hasn't been filtered through an arduous refining process, vernacular expression usually reveals oddities that are naive or amusing or peculiar as well as inventive. But the deciphering of the imperfect expression may heighten awareness in the receiver and even yield a superior message transmission.

To form speech or a visual image from scratch requires basic creativity and resourcefulness; to receive such a message requires creativity

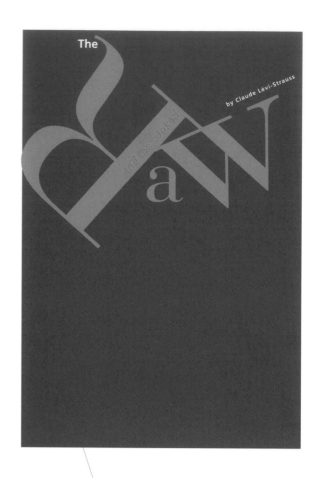

The
aw
by Claude Lévi-Strauss

u

t

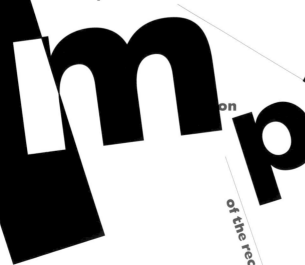

imprOmp

on

the
part

of the receiver.

Timing is a key dimension of speech.

How words are delivered—the pauses, the hesitations, the changes in tempo and inflection from deliberative to staccato, whispered to shouted—influences communication. Spontaneous communication is constantly adjusting to its context, looking for the appropriate form. It has a one-of-a-kind validity that only sophisticated acting can match.

Another aspect of timing is the synchronicity function of the mind, in which the mind's ability to merge idea and word creates gusts of awareness and sensitivity.

The tolerance for audacity and candor—frankness, sincerity, lack of affection—tends also to increase, contributing to the freshness of expression. Appropriateness (propriety) may be sacrificed, too. Design means sensing appropriateness, also sensing the degree of informality permitted.

Appropriateness alone as a measure, meaning merely proper or correct, can yield uninteresting results and ineffective communication. **When we express ourselves either verbally or visually in "real time" the resulting spontaneity reveals inevitable errors.** Extensive back tracking or editing is not possible. As listeners we are also more tolerant of error during "live" statements. Inflection and humor give a quality often missing in more sophisticated expressions.

The fetishes, the strict rules, of grammarians intrude on and often destroy vernacular expression. **The sense of the message rather than its technical correctness is more important.**

Simple misspellings can make humorous or serious changes in meaning. As faux pas they may contribute to the charm of the message. Amplified, they can become a language in their own right, as shown by James Joyce.

Blue Comet

The Blue Comet Diner sign is entropically afflicted. **Is "sickness" or "infection" another aspect of daily existence typical of vernacular?** Here entropy is combined with the vernacular of neon to lift it out of the ordinary, breaking the symmetry, creating another "aura."

Hair Jose Hair

Is it Hair Jose or Jose Hair? Hair Jose, worded intuitively rather than grammatically, as in the conventional sign at right, is probably a better name. And where is this place? The mix of Spanish, French, and English creates a noncommittal hybrid **like a novice in a foreign culture who can't hold to a single language.** Actually this is Rome! And the wavy grillwork strands of the gate say it all.

Grammatical Slips

Condensing language has its hazards. Usually we know what's meant even if there are gaps or transpositions or other grammatical errors. The texts of these ads retain their vernacular innocence as part of arriving at maximum economy of language. We have no trouble getting the intended messages, but they come with a dose of jocularity to boot. When "high" design attempts this kind of humor, it is correctly considered a failure.

Lost: small apricot poodle. Reward. Neutered. Like one of the family.

A superb and inexpensive restaurant. Fine food expertly served by waitresses in appetizing forms.

Dinner Special — Turkey $2.35; Chicken or Beef $2.25; Children $2.00.

For sale: an antique desk suitable for lady with thick legs and large drawers.

Four-poster bed, 101 years old. Perfect for antique lover.

Now is your chance to have your ears pierced and get an extra pair to take home, too.

Tired of cleaning yourself? Let me do it.

Dog for sale: eats anything and is fond of children.

Vacation Special: have your home exterminated.

Sheer stockings. Designed for fancy dress, but so serviceable that lots of women wear nothing else.

Stock up and save. Limit: one.

Wanted. Man to take care of cow that does not smoke or drink.

3-year-old teacher needed for pre-school. Experience preferred.

Auto Repair Service. Free pick-up and delivery. Try us once, you'll never go anywhere again.

Mixing bowl set designed to please a cook with round bottom for efficient beating.

economy... (and structure!)

Everyday language can be pithy and devoid of superfluity (as well as chatty and digressive). Vernacular, on one hand, is antiprofessional; on the other, any profession develops its own vernacular, a crude shorthand. Familiarity breeds a lingo based on sophistication and reverting to crudity. We tend to be impatient with flowery speech. But the same thing happens when abbreviation modifies specialized, in-group language. We try to avoid awkward repetition, especially of complex forms. Shortcuts connote familiarity. Anyone who uses the whole form is immediately pegged as an outsider.

I heard the waitress at a lunch counter ask if I wanted "maynze" with my sandwich.
"Maynze?" I said.
"Yeah, maynze."
...... "Oh, mayonnaise," I said.
"Yeah, what did I say?"
"You said 'maynze,'
......but you say it all the time, so naturally it gets a little clipped."

"Say, what are you, a teacher or somethin— ???
          ......O, that's o.k., they're not all bad!"

From a "low" standpoint, "high" is bad!

Ranzo Dock
The vernacular sometimes knows better what needs to be emphasized. In the context of a shoreline with few competing messages, the stripes on the dock pilings are more significant than the name of the stop, maintaining the abstract serenity of the environment.

▼ *"Alert Eyes See Lies"*
In the example, the poster message "Alert Eyes Read the NZT" (a newspaper) was painted over and replaced with "Alert Eyes See Lies" on the occasion of a chemical spill in the Rhine River, a scandal covered up by the chemical company responsible. The hand painting redirects the message and magnifies its urgency. **Immediacy and urgency are special provinces of the vernacular.**

In the vernacular of everyday spoken language we hear the
inflection of the voice. Inflection, by adding meaning to a
spoken phrase or sentence, makes the economy of idiomatic
expression possible. Foreigners hearing idiomatic phrases
will likely get a sense of the meaning through the inflection
even if they cannot fully understand the meaning of the
words. (Pithy, catchy idiomatic expressions, while useful for
casual speech, harbor in themselves the danger of the epithet

 —a label that unfairly and summarily
characterize a person or class of people, such
as this "Sambo" image for blacks, that is
very difficult to erase.)

Considering the casual, impromptu quality of vernacular, we
are tempted to think of it as antithetical to structure, yet it is
precisely the structuring process that makes a vernacular
expression a message. Structure holds it together. Deciphering the structure of vernacular expressions is revealing,
as we see in these examples.

Pithy Idioms

Idiomatic expressions are examples
of the efficiency of pithy expression for
frequent and general use. **These
expressions become part of
a society's vocabulary because they
are more picturesque and work
better in casual conversation than
their "correct" equivalents.**
They wouldn't work if they weren't
structurally clear; that is, if the relation of
sounds, syllables, and metaphor
weren't clear and fluid.
A few of many idiomatic expressions in
American English:
**all thumbs
have the blues
bug**

**buzz off
get carried away
cool
cool it
fly by night
fall apart
hit it off
in a pinch
knock oneself out
off the top of your head
out of the blue
play it by ear
pull one's leg
stick-in-the-mud
up in the air**

▲ *Nut Vendor, Crete*

**Bilateral symmetry seems to be the
default structure for most persons
untrained in design**. It is safe and
connotes order, but centering things, as
a recipe for design, is antithetical to the
discovery of a dynamic placement. In
this picture of nuts in a vendor's wagon
on the island of Crete, symmetry is a
logical way to divide the two kinds of
nuts. What makes the situation so
agreeable is how the symmetry is broken
by differentiating the number style. The
inverted logic of number size contributes
a quirkiness.

Solola Storefront, Guatemala ▶

Symmetry lends character to this modest Guatemalan grocery. The arrangement of the iconic paintings of food is **dynamic within its austere limits.**

"we don't talk" Service ▶

Does someone who scrawls a commitment to service convince customers of the quality of that service? **Though we may like the message for its content, its incongruous form makes it suspect and ironic.** The quotation marks, an immediate sign of semiliteracy and subject of ridicule, are precisely the source of interest. Why? Could it be because there is a certain logic in associating quotation marks with the word *talk*? Or do we like the inference that they get down to work without a lot of distracting chatter?

Rest Rooms ▲

Vernacular expression tends to be maker-oriented rather than public-oriented. The handmade adds personality; it is void of intimidation. This is its appeal and charm—and danger. **While crudity, artlessness (from a conventional aesthetic viewpoint), even ugliness combine to yield accessibility in an important sense, their peculiar quality results in a kind of infotainment.** Accessibility is more like theater; we play along with the act as such. Consequently, however, the response may stop with empathy, and that is not the intention. This is the danger in any communication that relies on humor: the joke comes across (to use the idiom); the message is missed.

Worms Sign, Pennsylvania ▲
Undulating letters and contrasting
weight combine—in a sense—
the cross-section of the worm with its
crawling. **The signmaker,
subconsciously or not, avoided
the easy convention of an
emphasized initial letter,** making
this into a more sophisticated
statement that bears refinement.
                                    ▼

Look beyond the surface crudity to the logic: **descending size of numerals in relation to their relative economic value.**
Can the idiosyncratic be applied more generally? In this case, the concept can be formalized as illustrated in the pure type versions. Clarity increases above $1.00.

.2^7 $_9$

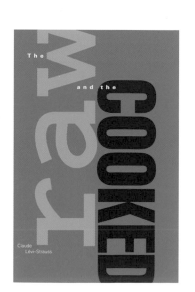

The raw and the COOKED

Claude
Lévi-Strauss

1.2^7 / $_9$

Handwriting is a quintessential example of vernacular expression. Simulated handwriting in commerce is often intended to suggest the personal even though it is reproduced by a mechanical process. But the other, less deceptive potential is that handwriting is a source for the evolution of newfound form.

Faked handwriting, fake one-of-a-kind handcraft, design by recipe, clip art dependence—these pervasive tendencies are essentially exploitive. For designers working with multiples produced by reproduction processes, conceiving the reproduction as the original— the ultimate manifestation of the creative process—is the creative challenge. It is made more difficult because of popular demand for things to look handmade or natural even when they are not.

Then and Now
....
Handwriting is a cultural phenomenon. The discipline and pride in handwriting exhibited in this sample from the late nineteenth century contrasted with the scribbled writing common in the late twentieth.

Khyber Pass
....
Writing time and place information on a mass-produced poster is an **authentic use of the handwritten.**

Market research becomes a mechanism to create a fit between product and demand. **In catering to audiences, it is common practice to use fakery to give a feeling of the personal while masking a wholly impersonal substrate.** The honesty of a communication or product is at risk. Honesty is the basis for trust and in turn for society.

We as designers, as representatives of the user, need to be satisfied that a communication or product is something we ourselves can strongly and genuinely support. To do this we need the necessary information, feeling, and intelligence to put things together. It means an ability to switch roles and sacrifice our ego-attachment to imposing or exotic "high" forms that may actually have "leaky roofs."

"John!" Brochure ▲

Comics have a special proximity to banal popular culture and are agents for the vernacular. In the accident prevention brochure, vernacular speech and the device of the speech balloon originating in the comics fuse with high design to address life-threatening situations. **The approach is to use humor and common speech but to walk the fine edge that prevents the message from being taken as a joke.**

▲ *Litterbug*

The litterbug sign, relying on the language of the comics but **failing to achieve a "high" resolution, is guilty** of the practice it condemns—creating visual litter.

Much design we see today is only chaotic, often justified by the theories of postmodernism and poststructuralism in which clarity is sacrificed for an intentional ambiguity. Though based in popular culture, these theories as applied are nevertheless often alienating to the ordinary person. Could this approach ever really work for an uninitiated public? The answer is not so simple, since communication, to be effective, challenges popular notions and awakens the mind to ask questions. There is a fine line between fresh innovation and chaotic, obscuring layering.

The possibilities available today for amplifying or dramatizing form present a special danger. The mechanical extension of "low" forms can command attention by the forms' sheer magnitude, volume, or dramatic force—independent of their content. We are easily duped by media magnification. As Marshall McLuhan observed in 1970:

"First American jazz and now the English Beatles have mechanically extended speech modes of the lower middle classes with image-acceptance. . . . such mimetic enlargements of ordinary experience are as enticing and flattering clichés as the movie or the motor car."

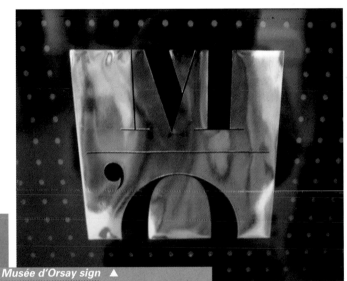

▲ AA Snack

In the case of the American Airlines snack, only the box follows the AA corporate identity. It contains **an odd assortment of generic and other miscellaneous identities, giving the whole package a "low" and informal quality**. The strategy is economically determined; more explicit identification is not needed because the audience is captive. We are probably relieved that the logo is not plastered repetitively on every piece. There is a fine line between corporate image enhancement and overkill.

Musée d'Orsay sign ▲

Vernacularization is a process by which "high" design is brought down. The Musée d'Orsay sign's polished reflectivity vernacularizes it— makes it common and accessible—by reflecting the viewer and crossing the line between it and the viewer.

Cultural and context
physical

Context in the realm of the vernacular, no less here than in any aspect of communication, plays the crucial role.

The 27.9 gas sign on page 208, for example, is immediately interesting from a safe distance. But would a person who doesn't have a personal relationship with this station trust it? Would a stranger choose it over a more "polished" establishment? Regarding the "we don't talk" service sign on page 206, does someone who scrawls a message of service convince of the quality of the service? We like the message for its content, but the incongruous form makes it suspect and ironic.

▼ High/Low Graffiti
The example of graffiti on the walls of an art school is influenced by a "high" form of drawing, cubism, in turn influenced by the "low" forms of vernacular "street graffiti." In its relative crudity and spontaneity it is recognized as "low"; in its stylistic derivation, it is **specific to its subculture of the world of modern art**. The example suggests that allocating a specific place for student graffiti—one voice at a time—could yield a compromising proportion between the ephemeral vernacular and the durational environment.

Frank's Sodas ▼
The soda sign painted at the entrance to a refreshment stand, by contrast, is recognized as vernacular in its naive and penetrating simplicity, its **handmade quality pushed to a "high" level of refinement.**

▲ 39¢ a Pot
The plant price sign shows a **congenial relationship among the factors of its support (wood), its shape (soft), the writing (organic and fast), the price (low), and the subject (flowers).** Farmers' markets are frequently good places to observe vernacular sign making.

These expressions are one of a kind. To reproduce them unchanged—putting them in another context—would alter their uniqueness, would in fact be antithetical to it.

Some vernacular expressions do endure in a way similar to folk music or fables, which gradually acquire form while preserving intensity and emotion. They stem from the grass-roots to form a groundswell of popular language including encoded styles or idioms. Having begun archetypally, their popularity lead almost inevitably to the cliché.

Regarding the interrelation of popular expression, cliché, and manipulation, Natalia Ilyin says:

"Vernacular refers to the language of the popular, it refers to the grassroots, to the natural groundswell of public opinion or discourse. This is the true vernacular. Yet it can also be used to mean the encoded style of that groundswell: the 50's Chevy, the type on the diner menu. We invoke the vernacular when we speak of the media, of print, radio, and television. The diner menu and the mediated image, though they speak to and of the average person, are, in reality, controlled by a culturally select group of individuals who decide who will see what, where. This is as it must be. We can't all get up there and man the radio towers. And much of this exploitation is not conscious. Yet a problem of representation and values remains: we romanticize the true vernacular as the language of the noble savage, we wrest it from its contextual surroundings, we destroy its legitimacy."

Trash ▲ ▲

Trash barrels on construction sites warrant little attention to their form or location. They are presumably of short duration, part of a chaotic environment. Both of these images evoke a kind of spontaneously generated (unintentionally, we guess) sense of being put away, **a falling motion germane to the subject.** The visually evident haste in writing *trash* adds meaning to the word.

Political Graffiti ▲

These examples of political graffiti, as compared to the kind of graffiti we see most commonly in American culture—personal signatures as ego gratification—promote political parties and **have larger communal reasons for being.**
Like the vernacular building architecture of the region, the Greek messages follow the terrain. The sign found in Guatemala respects the terrain of the rocks.

Claude Lévi-Strauss

Folk art, abstraction, and commonality

In thinking about the personal aspect of vernacular expression, we might look at folk art as a model. Much vernacular expression is folk art; all vernacular expression has personality and directness shared by folk art.

Vernacular expression at its best functions as folk art. According to Henry Glassie,

"Folk art is a critical weapon; it is a corrective concept, balancing the personal with the social, the progressive with the traditional, the novel with the perfect, the material with the spiritual. . . . Folk art is a reaction to simplification and error. It is one way we battle with our own culture, retarding its drive toward consolidation around falsehood."

Glassie describes the integrity, or naturalness, of folk art expression and how craftworkers naturally internalize a medium of expression, as in this example of Turkish rug weavers:

"Again and again I asked weavers in Turkey when they learned. The hesitancy and misdirection in their answers show the question to be wrong. As babies they crawled around the loom, listening to the soft sounds of the weft being pounded, watching designs rise wondrously on the warp, playing with scraps of brightly colored wool. As little girls they sat by their mothers, attending casually between fits of play in the sunshine. As bigger girls their curiosity increased and before they were twelve they were seated to the left of a master, their mother or an older sister, expertly doing their part, copying, repeating, receiving random hints about how to better their performance, until at last they had so mastered the art that they could control the progress of the rug, while guiding the younger weaver seated at the left."

▲ **Petroglyphs**

Petroglyphs reflect a combination of spontaneity, media expression, and traditional vernacular signs. **The superimposed language of letter forms draws from the source in several ways, keeping its own integrity.**

Folk art and literature, Glassie observes, orient toward the abstract; they are based more on types than on specific people. The audience recognizes these types, so more can be left implicit. **"The less we know and trust the people we are trying to reach, the more detail we put in the stories and pictures."**

Bernard Rudofsky finds the lessons of vernacular architecture to be:

— a fit to natural surroundings, often not easy terrain;
— insights into problems of living, rare good sense (v. business and prestige); and
— humaneness creating oases, not deserts.

"By dint of logic, life in old-world communities is singularly privileged. Instead of several hours of daily travel, only a flight of steps may separate a man's workshop or study from his living quarters. Since he himself helped to shape and preserve his environment, he never seems to tire of it."

Rudofsky quotes the historian Johan Huizinga as saying, "The expectation that every new discovery or refinement of existing means must contain the promise of higher values or greater happiness is an extremely naive thought. . . . It is not in the least paradoxical to say that a culture may founder on real and tangible progress."

As has been by now generally observed, the speed-up of information movement and the consequent inflation of cultural currency has a deleterious effect on established patterns, no matter how worth preserving they may be. Even if information transfer creates awareness of old or extra-cultural patterns of enduring value, the mere cloning of these patterns is a culturally empty pursuit.

common base,
w i d e
l a t i t u d e

Folk expression is reliant on a thread of of continuity over time, on a commonly understood history. The more broadly accepted the understanding, the greater the latitude for nuance. It is the uniqueness within the context of the base that gives personality and charm.

Snowman ▶

The base of three round balls stacked is from the vernacular. So are the facial features—eyes, nose, and mouth. Makers will be more or less inventive within those parameters. The parameters (based on the logic of the weight of each unit in relation to the height, to resistance to falling over, to melting, and on the anthropomorphic equivalent of being anchored in the legs, the roundness of the belly and head) are **abstract and open enough to permit free interpretation**. The example shown"obeys" the vernacular; also, in a simple effort to create a strong, clear image, its maker has instinctively used a specific complementary relationship (red-green) in the added elements, and a secondary complementary relationship (orange-blue in the sprayed-on food coloring). A synthesis with a unique stance and personality is achieved.

Barber Pole ▲

It stands in a residential district in Santa Fe, merges the decorative vernacular style of the region with the vernacular barber pole. Its pragmatic efficiency is heightened by the general sparseness of signs in the immediate environment. Is this **really** a barber shop?

The

Claude Lévi–Strauss

and the cooked

Speech is an act of distinguishing the unusual from the usual. This in essence is what we need and desire as an outcome in communication. Personal stories told simply and naturally have a certain special validity we do not always recognize. Folk forms developed as individual stories gain wider social recognition and empathy.

The cultivation of storytelling has a beneficial effect on maintaining a sense of the real and comprehensible. This has already been demonstrated in chapter 4 on mapping. Doodling and daydreaming are free-associative ways of storytelling that can be exceedingly productive for the imagination.

Puns are products of spontaneously generated crossovers, a kind of real-time collaging. The language expert H. W. Fowler says about the subject:

"The assumption that puns are per se contemptible, betrayed by the habit of describing every pun not as a pun, but as a bad pun or a feeble pun, is a sign at once of sheepish docility and desire to seem superior. Puns are good, bad, or indifferent, and only those who lack the wit to make them are unaware of the fact."

Avital Ronell, the ultimate purveyor of puns in the grand manner, quotes from Michel Corbin, "The pun is a stretched tautology, shimmering with meaning, an explosive incantation which plays upon repetition all the better to destroy it, and drags the mind along the slope of the Same the better to leave room for the break-in of the Other."

She calls Noah Jacobs's (*Naming Day in Eden*) formulation "gelastic":

"The Janus word makes of human speech a slippery instrument. It is, however, the reflection of the double nature of man himself, of the contradiction that lies at the very heart of humanity. In Eden man knew no ambiguity, but when he fell, he became Janus-faced, a parvus-mundus of opposites, perilously poised at the juncture of nature and spirit, the riddle of the crossroads, the glory and the jest of the world."

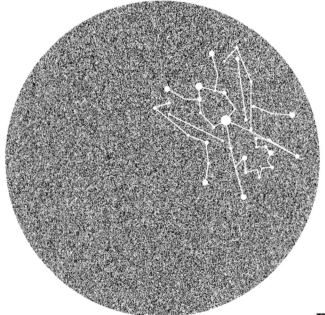

▲ **Fly by Night**
A fly-by-night operation, as evasive as the identification of a celestial constellation.

▲ **(rumored to be something)**
We can only guess at the meaning, but this visual "rumor" suggests a sign quality most commercial graphics lack, and as integration with its local environment it teaches a lesson.

Rumor, one of the faults of popular discourse (popular being another aspect of the vernacular of a given culture), can have another side. Not that rumormongering should be promoted, but the reaction to rumor can be, in Martin Heidegger's terms, an enabler. Whatever rumor's outward absurdity, it often stems from an underlying truth. As Ronell writes:

"Heidegger tells us . . . that rumor is essentially related to the most daring thinking. Or rather, a daring writing enjoys a relationship of enslavement to something like rumor, utterance's murky rumbling . . . the dared word, in its anteriority, has been open to rumor, which acts as the horizon to all language testing. While still under the shadow of negativity, rumor nonetheless acts as the enabler, the ground and horizon for the founding of a 'more original and more careful thinking.' "

Ronell points out that rumors communicate, like certain diseases, a kind of uncontrollable contagion that leaks out. The aims and precise expression of these utterances are not imputable to any knowable origin. They have no identifiable creator, and yet rumors are stated as if they revealed truth. Rumors are "a variety of speech act that is always on the run, existing in the mode of a hit-and-run temporality, coming, like a sudden accident, from nowhere." The underlying truth needs to be discerned.

Puns, rumors, doodles, though they add chaos to experience, can induce heightened acuity.

▼ **Doodle**
Doodling and daydreaming, when a kind of unpressured playing that **releases subconscious energy,** help release the uninhibited and untried.

The raw

The raw and the Cooked

raw raw raw raw raw raw raw raw raw raw raw raw raw raw raw raw raw raw raw raw raw raw raw raw raw raw raw raw raw raw raw raw raw raw raw raw raw raw raw raw raw raw raw raw raw raw raw raw raw raw raw raw

by Claude Lévi-Strauss

The appropriate and genuine interfusing of high and low design is a desirable, albeit elusive, goal.

The Source's Apprentice

Graphic design is the meeting ground where content from diverse outside sources meets the language of abstract form to create communication. In these projects we have drawn from diverse content domains and explored how the content infuses the form-making process and, reciprocally, the way graphic form can aid in communication. As I hope you have seen, contending with new content can charge us with new energy and expressive means. It also brings with it its own criteria for expression. The fusion of the language of visual design with another source is a way of progressive broadening in education. Besides the rich variation potential in graphic form language in and of itself, combination with other languages compounds this potential.

In "apprenticing ourselves" to these outside sources we also need to know our limits. In Paul Dukas's *Sorcerer's Apprentice*, a magician's assistant, in his master's absence, repeats a magic formula he has heard his master use. The magic words bring a broomstick to life. He commands it to carry water from the well. It obeys perfectly. But when the task is completed the broomstick does not stop; it continues to carry bucket after bucket of water until the room is flooded. In desperation, the apprentice cuts the broomstick in two, but to his amazement each half now carries water. It is not until the sorcerer himself returns and says other magic words that the action stops.

It is possible through teaching or through any kind of exposure to open a floodgate of action that we are helpless to control or resolve. We open the way through endless experimentation, through exposure to myriad styles of work, or through application of morphologies to the boundless possibilities for design.

Without the ability to end the process, to focus it, to say "enough!" this is dangerous knowledge. To learn to overcome the dangers, it is good and useful to structure progressive probes at expanding our language and sources until we become masters who know enough to fill the reservoir but prevent the destructive flood.

- Graphic design has an aesthetic potential. The place of education, whether in school or of oneself—the ongoing saga—is to elevate standards for professional practice by showing that problem-solving never precludes an aesthetically based solution. Graphic design, creating interfaces in interdisciplinary and collaborative contexts, crosses boundaries to draw from sources outside itself and creates an aesthetic in its synthesizing function. In this multiplicity lies the very excitement of being a designer. Education for design consists in preparation for the personal contribution to this activity filled with the unexpected.

The boundaries to be crossed are many, of which this set of explorations gives the merest hint.

Students contributing their work to this volume are listed below.

Chapter 1

p.18, calendar:
Yumiko Shoto
p.20, cyberspace:
JooYoun Hong
p.21, lion:
Gregg Robinson
p.24, Mahler interpretation:
JooYoun Hong
p.26, dialogue/discourse:
Diana Cadwalader
pp.28–31, *I Ching*
interpretation:
Mi Kyung Lee

Chapter 2

pp.51, 54–61 hand icon
and development:
Alexandra Weil
pp.52–53, icons row 1:
Amy Grove
Mark Beckwith
George Plesko
James Hiesener
Sonali Nande
Kara Hannon
Sylvio Napoleone
Shushi Yoshinaga
row 2:
Lynn Fylak
Mark Jones
Vaishali Nande
JudyAnn Elias
Kathleen Whalen
Lyda Heller
Sheri Kriebel
Nancy Neducsin
row 3:
Maria Kerdel
Robert Wente
Alexandra Weil
Louise Comey
Denise Shedro
Sun Jung
Gregg Robinson
Carol Kinderman
row 4:
Christy Verna
Christopher Peterson
Laurie Frick
Kristen Bower
Richard Conway
Frank Marchese
Rebekah Schmidt
Ross Levine
row 5:
Mi Kyung Lee
Melissa Squillante
Mychele Lepinsky
Gorete Ferreira dos Passos
Wendy Garfinkel
Michael Aregood
Myung You Oh
Agnieszka Swigoniak
p.58, headdress:
Louise Comey
pp.62–63, row 1:
Alexandra Weil
Mi Kyung Lee
Suzanne Guelli
row 2:
Carol Kindermann
Shushi Yoshinaga
Wendy Garfinkel

pp. 64–65:
row 1:
Alexandra Weil
Julie Colton
George Plesko
row 2:
Carol Kinderman
Kristen Bower
Diana Gaspero
Mychele Lepinsky
pp.66–67, snake:
Wendy Garfinkel
pp.68–69, fairy:
Kathleen Whalen
pp.70–71, pen:
Ross Levine
pp.72–79, road:
Mi Kyung Lee
pp.80–83, syringe:
Myung You Oh
pp.84–90, clown:
Vaishali Nande

Chapter 3

pp.92–93:
John Burns
pp.94, 97–101:
Jennifer Long
pp. 95, 102–103:
George Plesko
pp.104–105:
Bernadette Rivell
pp.106–107:
David Matthai
pp.108–109,
clockwise from lower left:
Armena Jehanian
Sonali Nande
Gorete Ferreira dos Passos
Kristen Bower
p.110:
Agnieszka Swigoniak
Cynthia Cheatham
Kim Mollo
p.111:
Kara Hannon
Sonali Nande
p.112:
Kristen Bower
p.113:
Kara Hannon
Gorete Ferreira dos Passos
p.114:
Sang Lee
Kim Mollo
p.115:
Stacey Byrd
Christopher Peterson
p.117:
Lora Winslow
p.118:
James Hiesener
Nancy Neducsin
Alexandra Weil
p.119:
Ross Levine
Amy Grove
Shushi Yoshinaga
Wendy Garfinkel
p.120:
James Hiesener
Nancy Neducsin
Sylvio Napoleone
Alexandra Weil
p.121:
Mi Kyung Lee
Wendy Garfinkel
Shushi Yoshinaga
Jennifer Detwiler

p.122:
James Hiesener
JooYoun Hong
Kathleen Whalen
Bernadette Rivell
p.123:
Laura Chambers
Ross Levine
Dorothy Funderwhite
Amy Grove
p.124:
Jennifer Detwiler
Kathleen Whalen
Jennifer Long
Jeffrey Kasner
p.125:
Mark Beckwith
Dana DiPaulo
Mychele Lepinsky
Myung You Oh
p.126:
Suzanne Guelli

Chapter 4

pp.130–139:
Maria Kerdel
pp.140–141:
Kara Hannon
pp.142–143:
Laurie Frick
pp.144–145:
Jose Cacho
pp.146–147:
Vaishali Nande
pp.148–149:
Richard Conway
p.150:
Melissa Squillante
p.151:
Agnieszka Swigoniak
p.152:
Margo Borten

Chapter 5

pp.156–57, top:
Wendy Garfinkel
bottom:
Dana DiPaulo
pp.158–159, top:
David Lee
bottom:
Amy Grove
pp.160–161, top:
Shushi Yoshinaga
bottom:
Laura Chambers
pp.162–163:
Jennifer Detwiler
p.164:
JooYoun Hong

Chapter 6

p.169, four restaurants:
Alexandra Weil
pp.170–71:
dentist:
JooYoun Hong
architect:
Myung You Oh
rock musician:
Ross Levine
philosopher:
Jennifer Detwiler
archaeologist:
Dana DiPaulo
astronomer:
Julie Colton

Chapter 7

p.197, raw/cooked:
Natalie Kornbluh
Brad Bookler
p.198:
Kara Hannon
Sonali Nande
Agnieszka Swigoniak
Armena Jehanian
Gorete Ferreira dos Passos
Alicia Sinha
p.200–201:
David Lee
p.202:
raw/cooked:
Inessa Skorodinsky
impromptu:
Sonali Nande
p.205, diner photo:
Susan Fritz
p.205, sambo icon:
Enrique Jones II
p.207, raw/cooked:
Justyna Jagielka
p.208, raw/cooked:
Tom Neufeld
p.213, raw/cooked:
Myung You Oh
p.214, petroglyphs:
Kara Hannon
p.216, raw/cooked:
Bruce RanSone
p.217, raw/cooked:
Sonia Mercado
p.218, fly by night:
Julle Colton
p.220, raw/cooked:
Robert Chacko

Quotations from other sources:

Introduction

9   Karrie Jacobs, *Metropolis*, 1990, as
    quoted in *Spirals: Book Six, Graphic
    Design History* (Providence: Rhode
    Island School of Design, 1991), 225
9   Jeanne Bamberger, Symposium on
    Cybernetics, The University of the Arts,
    1994
11   Jim Thomas, internet post, Carnegie
    Mellon University, course notes for
    SOCI 675 (jthomas@sun.soci.niu.edu)
    Jerome Bruner, *The Process of Education*
    (Cambridge: Harvard University Press,
    1960), 7–12
    Jasper Morrison quoted in Melissa E.
    Bigg, "Spare Parts," *Metropolis* (July–
    August 1994), 71
12   *Armin Hofmann: His Work, Quest and
    Philosophy* (Basel: Birkhäuser,1989)
    Museum of Design, Zürich, exhibition
    flyer, 1990
    Stephan Wolpe, "Lecture on Dada,"
    Musical Quarterly 72, no. 2 (1986), 205
13   Jeremy Campbell, *Grammatical Man*
    (New York: Simon and Schuster, 1982),
    216
    Herbert Muschamp, "A Philadelphia
    Show Evokes Kahn's Tough Poetry,"
    New York Times, October 7, 1991
    Ned Rorem, "The Double Identity of Ned
    Rorem" by John Mascaro, *Applause*,
    April 1989, 218
    Margaret Yourçenar, *The Memoirs of
    Hadrian* (Hammondsworth: Penguin,
    1978), 39
    Italo Calvino, *Six Memos for the Next
    Millennium* (Cambridge: Harvard
    University Press, 1988)
14   Jeremy Campbell (play), *Grammatical
    Man*, 144
15   Jeremy Campbell (complexity),
    Grammatical Man, 102

Chapter 1

16   Paul Klee, *Tagebücher* (Stuttgart:
    Deutscher Bücherbund, 1957), 69
    John Dewey, *Experience and Nature*
    (Chicago: Open Court, 1926), 81–82
17   cognitive map of the cosmos, *Parabola*
    (August 1993), inside cover
    Note to the Chuckchi diagram:
    "The feature which characterizes sym-
    bolism is precisely that the thing which
    later reflection calls a symbol is not a
    symbol, but a direct vehicle, a concrete
    embodiment, a vital incarnation . . . .
    Symbolism in this sense dominates
    not only all early art and cult but social
    organization as well. Rites, designs,
    patterns are all charged with a signifi-
    cance which we may call mystic, but
    which is immediate and direct to those
    who have and celebrate them. Be the
    origin of the totem what it may, it is
    not a cold, intellectual sign of a social
    organization; it is that organization
    made present and visible, a center of
    emotionally charged behavior."
    (Dewey, *Experience and Nature*, 81-82)
    Ezio Manzini, from "Prometheus of the
    Everyday: The Ecology of the Artificial
    and the Designer's Responsibility,"
    Design Issues (Fall 1992), trans. John
    Cullars

23   untitled offset lithograph,"K" (student
    magazine, School of Design, Basel,
    1963)
28–29 adapted from Richard Wilhelm, *I Ching,
    or The Book of Changes*, trans.
    Cary F. Baynes (Princeton, N.J.:
    Princeton University Press, 1967), and
    I Ching, trans. James Legge, ed.
    with intro. Ch'u Chai and Winberg Chai
    (Hyde Park, N.Y.: University Books,
    1964)

Chapter 2

51   Kenneth J. Hiebert quoted in
    universal/Unique, exhibition catalog
    (University of the Arts, 1988), 30

Chapter 3

92   Kenneth J. Hiebert quoted in exhibition
    "Twelve Eclipses," Mythos Festival
    exhibition, University of the Arts, 1991
93   Susanne K. Langer, *Mind: An Essay on
    Human Feeling*, vol. 1 (Baltimore:
    Johns Hopkins University Press, 1967),
    187ff.
94   Carl Orff and Gunild Keetman, *Music for
    Children*, Angel Records, LP-3582
95   Langer, *Mind*, 185
108   Orff/Keetman, *Music for Children*
110   David Lewiston, *Music from the Morning
    of the World*, Nonesuch CD-H-72015,
    1900
114   Kronos Quartet, *Black Angels*, Electra
    Nonesuch, CD-979242-1, 1990
116   Hildegard von Bingen, *Symphoniae*,
    Sequentia Ensemble, Harmoni Mundi
    CD-77020-2-RG, 1985
    Ludwig van Beethoven, *Cello Sonatas*,
    Lynn Harrel, cello, and Vladimir
    Ashkenazy, piano, London CD-215379,
    1987
    Mickey Hart, *Planet Drum*, Rykodisc RCD-
    10206, 1991
    Music for Instruments and Computer,
    Experimental Music Studio, Media Lab,
    MIT, 1979
    Arvo Pärt, *Tabula Rasa*, liner notes, ©1984
    Wolfgang Sandner, ECM CD-1275,
    Munich: ECM Records, 1984
    Arvo Pärt, *Miserere*, ECM Records, CD-
    1430 GmbH, 1984
    Harvey Goldman and Warren Lehrer, *The
    Search for It and Other Pronouns*, LaLa
    Music, LLESCD001, 1991

Chapter 4
129   Edward R. Tufte, *The Visual Display of
    Quantitative Information* (Cheshire,
    Conn.: Graphics Press, 1983), 191

Chapter 5
154   Richard Saul Wurman, *What-If, Could-Be*
    (Philadelphia: Group for Environmental
    Education, 1976)
    Tufte, *Quantitative Information*, 13
    Worldwatch Papers published by
    Worldwatch Institute, Washingon, D.C.,
    1990

Chapter 6
166   Margaret Courtney-Clarke, *African
    Canvas* (New York: Rizzoli, 1990)

    Claude Lévi-Strauss, *Tristes Tropiques*,
    trans. John Russell (New York:
    Atheneum, 1961), 100
167   Robert Venturi, Denise Scott Brown, and
    Steven Izenour, *Learning from Las
    Vegas* (Cambridge: MIT Press, 1972), 1ff

Chapter 7

194   cat drawing by Stephanie Hiebert, age
    four
196   Immanuel Kant quoted in Avital Ronell,
    *Finitude's Score: Essays for the End of
    the Millenium* (Lincoln: University of
    Nebraska Press, 1994), 147
197   Claude Lévi-Strauss, *The Raw and the
    Cooked (Cru et le cuit)*, trans. John and
    Doreen Weightman (New York: Harper
    and Row, 1969)
198   Kathleen M. Carley and David S. Kaufer,
    "Semantic Connectivity: An Approach
    for Analyzing Symbols in Semantic
    Networks," *Communication Theory*
    (August, 1993), 183
199   clip art, Ann Gould, "Art on the Assembly
    Line," *Typographica* 12 (December
    1965), 41
    type styles, David Mayer, program notes,
    "Eisenstein's Potemkin: A Shot-by-
    Shot Presentation," Mann Music
    Center Concert Series, 1994
200   Natalia Ilyin, "Taking the Plunge," *Lift
    and Separate* (New York: Herb Lubalin
    Center, 1993), 61
202   Frances Butler, "Retarded Arts: The
    Failure of Fine Arts Education," *AIGA
    Journal* 13 (1995)
    Noam Chomsky's views described in
    Campbell, *Grammatical Man*, 160
203   grammatical slips, anonymous posting
    on the Internet
211   Marshall McLuhan, *From Cliché to
    Archetype* (New York: Viking, 1970),
    145
214   Henry Glassie, *The Spirit of Folk Art*, New
    York: Harry N. Abrams,1989), 254, 95
215   Bernard Rudofsky, *Architecture Without
    Architects* (New York: Museum of
    Modern Art, 1965), preface
218   Ronell, *Finitude's Score*, 86–94

Colophon

Unless otherwise attributed, all photographs,
  drawings, designs, and text are by the author
  © Kenneth J. Hiebert.

This book was composed principally in Adobe
  Univers and Garamond families and, in
  chapter 7, Gill Sans Extra Bold. Other fonts
  were used in examples.

Pages were composed by the author in QuarkXpress
  using image files prepared in Adobe Illustrator,
  Adobe Photoshop, Macromedia FreeHand, and
  MacroModel.

Digital file pre-press by Kenneth J. Hiebert.
Film production by Kalnin Graphics, Jenkintown,
  Pennsylvania.
Printed in Singapore by Imago.